Teaching
Young Adult
Literature

Other Titles by Author

Teaching Young Adult Literature Today: Insights, Considerations, and Perspectives for the Classroom Teacher

Young Adult Nonfiction: Gateway to the Common Core

Teaching
Young Adult
Literature

Integrating, Implementing, and
Re-Imagining the Common Core

Edited by Judith A. Hayn, Jeffrey S. Kaplan,
Amanda L. Nolen, and Heather A. Olvey

ROWMAN & LITTLEFIELD
Lanham • Boulder • New York • London

Published by Rowman & Littlefield
A wholly owned subsidiary of The Rowman & Littlefield Publishing Group, Inc.
4501 Forbes Boulevard, Suite 200, Lanham, Maryland 20706
www.rowman.com

Unit A, Whitacre Mews, 26-34 Stannary Street, London SE11 4AB

British Library Cataloguing in Publication Information Available

Library of Congress Cataloging-in-Publication Data Available

ISBN 978-1-4758-1301-2 (hardcover)
ISBN 978-1-4758-1302-9 (paperback)
ISBN 978-1-4758-1303-6 (e-book)

∞™ The paper used in this publication meets the minimum requirements of American National Standard for Information Sciences—Permanence of Paper for Printed Library Materials, ANSI/NISO Z39.48-1992.

Printed in the United States of America

To my father,
Guy R. Coonrod,
the teacher-educator

Contents

Preface

The Common Core State Standards (CCSS) define requirements for all educators to become literacy teachers. Since this responsibility no longer falls solely on the shoulders of English Language Arts (ELA) teachers, many other educators feel they lack the ability to teach literacy. The editors of this text and the authors who contributed to it believe that young adult literature (YAL) not only can help teachers from various content areas become more confident in their ability to teach literacy, but also can connect the standards to what is in these texts. Using YAL in all classes enables students to connect to what they are learning in more meaningful ways since this literature is written for adolescents while much of what we offer to middle and high school teens does not enable them to engage with text.

Teaching Young Adult Literature: Integrating, Implementing, and Re-Imagining the Common Core is intended as a primer for those teachers who are dealing with literacy instruction in content areas, including any educator who would like to learn more about the efficacy of YAL and how to teach it. The editors and chapter authors firmly believe that YAL offers a viable route for teaching content area literacy, as well as facilitating the CCSS. The chapters in the text are written by some of the country's leading literacy experts, and each chapter offers suggestions, strategies, and research-based advice for using YAL in the classroom to teach the standards while supplying the all-important links with students.

Introduction

The authors who contributed to this text believe that young adult literature (YAL) can meet the Common Core's push to include literacy across content areas, as well as meet the standards in creative and effective ways. This text is intended to give educators a resource to aid them in creating a literacy curriculum. The included chapters written by experts from different universities across the country offer a variety of methods for using YAL to meet the standards while connecting with students. Following a framework established in the first chapter introducing the importance of YAL and discussing its relevance, other authors tackle various ways to teach it. Although each chapter may suggest different strategies and the authors' rationale for utilizing YAL are different, each shares a common purpose with the others: to promote the efficacy of YAL to engage students while at the same time meeting the rigorous standards set forth by the Common Core.

Chapter 1 by Hayn, Layton, Nolen, and Olvey, titled "Content Area Literacy and Young Adult Literature: Examining the Landscape," discusses and explains the barriers to inclusion of YAL in curricula, and attempts to break those barriers down. The authors also offer suggestions for how to use YAL in content area classes. This chapter provides the framework for the rest of the text.

Hill and Clemmons discuss how to incorporate YAL into health science and also implement the standards in chapter 2, "Stimulating Health Dialogue and Evaluation: Implementations of Young Adult Literature to Address Common Core Standards in Health Classes." By using Angela Johnson's *First Part Last,* Chris Crutcher's *Staying Fat for Sarah Burns,* and Lara Halse Anderson's *Wintergirls,* the authors show how issues including teen pregnancy, building healthy relationships, and eating disorders can be examined in classrooms.

Text complexity is discussed and modeled by using two YA texts in chapter 3, "Knowing Readers and Knowing Books: Using Text Complexity Measures to Select Texts and Motivate Adolescent Readers," by Parsons and Bandré. Using Sally Gardner's *Maggot Moon* and Elizabeth Wein's *Code Name Verity* as models, the authors discuss different ways in which texts can be complex.

"Exploring Point of View and Narration in Young Adult Literature: Connecting Teen Readers with Multiple Narrator Books" by Young, Hadaway, and Ward (chapter 4) offers readers examples of YA texts that utilize different points of view to tell the stories. They include a discussion of the recent trend in YAL of having multiple narrators tell a single story; the authors tie up their chapter by connecting the standards to the texts they suggest.

Goering, Holland, and Connors demonstrate the use of YAL in teaching argumentative writing in the next chapter. Chapter 5, "Anchoring the Teaching of Argumentative Writing Units with Young Adult Literature," examines the authors' work in a collaborative writing project through the College Ready Writers Program, offering an analysis of their work in the classroom, as well as giving educators practical ideas for teaching argumentation. This project is based on John Corey Whaley's novel *Noggin,* but the projects they present can translate to other books and topics.

Chapter 6, "Using Young Adult Literature in Implementing Common Core Literacy Standards with Inclusion Students in Non-IDEA Classrooms," considers the need for inclusion-themed YAL. Hazlett and Sweeney discuss the standards and how they affect students with disabilities in non-IDEA classrooms, as well as the necessity for the portrayal of positive role models in literature for students with disabilities so that students of all abilities can understand and empathize with one another. The chapter is concluded with a list of inclusion-themed YAL titles.

Polleck discusses the value of book clubs in chapter 7, "Using Book Clubs and Adolescent Literature to Support the Common Core Standards." The author argues that book clubs offer a way to bring more YAL to teens' attention, and describes a yearlong study that was conducted in an urban high school where Polleck facilitated reading groups. The findings of this study show that adolescents enjoy engaging in book clubs.

In chapter 8, "Annotated Resources for the Classroom Teacher," Hayn, Layton, and Olvey use Bickmore and Emiraliyeva-Pitre's article "Teaching Diverse Young Adult Literature in Harmony with the Common Core State Standards: Is It Still Just about the Characters, the Plot, the Setting" as a framework for discussing the present-day educators' reality of balancing the CCSS with student engagement, and content area literacy. Resources for teachers are offered, along with YA texts listed by content area.

Chapter One

Content Area Literacy and Young Adult Literature

Examining the Landscape

Judith A. Hayn, Kent Layton, Amanda L. Nolen, and Heather A. Olvey

The emergence of young adult literature as offering a channel to improve content area literacy is a relatively new concept. Those of us who are committed to the field's relevance and usefulness emphasize that the classroom teacher needs to plan curriculum based firmly on the concept that YAL (young adult literature) has much to offer in improving and enhancing literacy skills.

Confusion and consternation occurs when differing attitudes and interpretations develop due to the imposition and requirements of standards-driven teaching. Whether these are the Common Core State Standards (CCSS), or state-imposed curriculum frameworks, the result is often the same. What can those of us who promote YAL as providing valid venues for meeting these standards do? How can we prove that adolescent literature gives legitimate choices for accomplishing literacy in English language arts and in the other content fields?

This concept of adolescent content literacy is reinforced by the National Governors Association's (2010) mandates for CCSS, which, ironically, do not prescribe nor mandate what should be taught:

> While the Standards focus on what is most essential, they do not describe all that can or should be taught. A great deal is left to the discretion of teachers and curriculum developers. The aim of the Standards is to articulate the fundamentals, not to set out an exhaustive list or a set of restrictions that limits what can be taught beyond what is specified herein. (p. 6)

1

Steadman, Carroll, and Froelich (2011/2012) remind us that the CCSS's assertion that content area teachers must share responsibility for teaching literacy skills is, however, not a new concept. Siebert and Draper (2008) report the notion that all teachers should be teachers of reading was discussed as far back as 1925.

Likewise, Gray (1952) remarked, "Learning to use the tools of reading to do the tasks required in the content field is comparable in many respects to the use of simple household tools to do a repair job" in his address to colleagues at the Fifteenth Annual Conference on Reading (p. 4). Since the CCSS reiterates the premise that literacy should be an integral component of all content areas, how can we take advantage of this emphasis and recommend YAL as having the tools to accomplish this?

This clamor for adolescent literacy development does not appear to result in evidence that contemporary teens are better readers than their earlier counterparts. In fact, Shanahan and Shanahan (2008) point out that the reverse is true. They cite National Assessment of Educational Progress data from 2007 as indicating that high school students score lower in reading than in 1922, while fewer high school students read at proficient levels and even more read at below-basic level.

"According to American College Testing (2006), the proportion of students on track for successful college work actually diminished as students advance through U.S. schools from eighth through twelfth grade" (p. 42). Though this data is nearly a decade old, the outlook today remains dismal. Clearly other approaches to dealing with adolescent literacy need to be explored.

BARRIERS TO YAL INCLUSION

Nonetheless, works that young adults and teens actually read receive negative feedback from critics and others. Stotsky (2010) concludes after examining high school curricular choices in high school English that "almost all the books [adolescents] read are relative easy to read" (p. 8). The CCSS revives the support for this accusation that YAL lacks rigor and complexity. Librarians and teachers who believe in and espouse the use of YAL because it connects with teens and their experiences need to counter these arguments by addressing them and providing access to connections with CCSS.

This chapter will discuss some of the additional barriers educators face in implementing YAL in content area classrooms, including the English language arts. The remaining chapters document the rationale for doing so and suggest multiple approaches in varied content area disciplines to accomplish the integration of YAL into literacy curriculum.

One of the primary difficulties in adding or infusing YAL into classrooms begins with high school English curriculum developers and teachers. Traditionally, English language arts teachers have been the primary literacy instructors, assuming responsibility for teaching reading and writing, along with speaking and listening. Convincing English teachers to include YAL in the high school curriculum has been a major stumbling block in getting these texts in the classroom.

There are many reasons for this hesitation to use YAL, two of which include the belief that either YAL is not literary enough, or that its use will incite the masses and anger parents. In an effort to avoid having to defend one's non-canonical choice of texts, educators fall back on the classics simply because it is easier to do.

Applebee's (1993) comprehensive study of texts commonly taught in high school English courses noted that the selections came only from the canon. Stotsky (2010) updated this survey and found that only one YAL text, *Speak* by Laurie Halse Anderson, appeared as one of the most frequently assigned works. "Teachers are torn between teaching the literature they feel will be most useful to their students and the literature that everyone else thinks they ought to teach" (Bushman & Hans, 2005, p. 167), which leads them to feeling guilty if they do not teach the classics.

Another barrier appears within the CCSS themselves. Although the document reiterates that teachers are responsible for selecting their own texts in the content areas, the publication provides exemplars that are primarily couched in the canon. Conners (2013) also notes the fact that *Speak* is the only YA book listed as complex enough to teach, and Miller (2014) points out that Marcus Zusak's *The Book Thief* is the only YA text for grades 9–10 that is considered as having comparable literary merit to the classics.

An ironic detail about including *The Book Thief* is that it is actually a cross-over that was originally sold as an adult book, so the exclusion of YA titles leads many teachers to believe that they are not allowed to teach YAL. The real fear is that school districts will mandate the use of these exemplars and nothing else, with teachers having limited input into which texts are taught. Conners and Shepard (2011/2012) provide anecdotal evidence that this phenomenon is occurring at the district and school level in a mid-Southern state that has committed to CCSS.

Another barrier to acceptance and access for using YAL in teaching content area literacy lies in the lack of research. Evidence that middle and secondary teacher educators are studying the impact of content area literacy with younger teens exists, but few have addressed the use of YAL. Shanahan and Shanahan (2008) in their article "Teaching Disciplinary Literacy to Adolescents: Rethinking Content-Area Literacy," designed a two-year study on disciplinary literacy to examine how secondary content teachers teach reading strategies to adolescents in their respective fields. Their findings suggest that different strategies might be indicated for math, chemistry, and history.

> More recent treatments and the data from this study suggest that as students move through school, reading and writing instruction should become increasingly disciplinary, reinforcing and supporting student performance with the kinds of texts and interpretive standards that are needed in the various disciplines or subjects. (p. 57)

Thomson (2011) also looked at how young adolescents were instructed in content area literacy in middle school social studies, science, and mathematics. In her qualitative study, she concludes that the school as a whole must support adolescent literacy development for it to be integrated as part of the culture.

It is a fact that students are expected to read and write across all of the content areas, and each subject has its own academic vocabulary and syntax that students must learn to navigate. For example, students cannot read a math text by skimming to gain a general idea of the content because even function words such as "the" mean something very specific (Shanahan & Shanahan, 2008). Social studies teachers often want students to question the credibility of the author so that biases can be understood since historians can have very different interpretations of past events.

Teaching students how to read different texts is critical to their education. The CCSS also push students toward using better critical thinking skills, and this must be accomplished through literacy skills as well. The problem lies in the fact that many adolescents are bored with what is currently being taught. It has been stated that North American English teachers "believe that 20 percent or less of their students read assigned books" (Kittle, 2013, p. 15).

Beach, Appleman, Hynds, and Wilhelm (2011) state that teens "often reject anything taught in a classroom, so what they choose to read for pleasure ends up being remote from what's available in a classroom or school library" (p. 79). Bushman and Hans (2005) interviewed and observed many adolescents in ELA classes and found overwhelmingly that the students did not connect to the canon. One student stated, "I love to read, but I hate literature" (p. 168), and when he was asked to elaborate he conveyed the idea that what he was being assigned to read in class had little, if anything, to do with him personally.

This lack of connection forces adolescents to either hate reading in general as they slog their way through texts they neither care about nor understand, or they stop reading the texts completely and rely on synopses either from *CliffsNotes*, or even verbally from their peers to get them through their classes

(Bushman and Hans, 2005). By relying solely on the canon in ELA classes, and only textbooks in other content areas, students are not learning to love reading, sharpening their critical thinking skills, or engaging with the content. Instead, they are learning to get by with doing as little as possible using summaries other people have written. This is not the engaging curriculum effective teachers want to promote, nor is it meeting the goals of the standards.

BREAKING DOWN THE BARRIERS

Empowering Educators

So, how can we justify the use of YAL in the face of the aforementioned barriers? With regards to high school English curriculum developers and teachers, education is key. Teachers of all content areas should familiarize themselves with current YA lit (Bickmore and Pitre, 2014; Winsor, 2013) by reading YA journals such as *The ALAN Review, JAAL,* and *SIGNAL,* in addition to reading various YA texts.

While award lists such as *YALSA* and the National Book Award nominees are excellent starting places, Beach, Appleman, Hynds, and Wilhelm (2011) note that these lists often differ from what teens themselves choose in lists such as *Teenreads*. An important thing for teachers to know is what their students are reading so that current interests can be integrated into the curriculum.

Bickmore and Pitre (2014) maintain that educators should become expert teachers and readers in the field of YAL, and can do so not only by reading the aforementioned journals and consulting awards lists, but also by becoming familiar with academic books about YAL, blogs and by attending conferences and/or workshops. They admit that one of the biggest keys to becoming an expert is to read YAL widely; however, it must be taken to an academic level of study in order to make that transition from novice to expert (p. 40). Perhaps by becoming more familiar with the genre, educators' perceptions of YAL will change from negative to positive.

The question of text complexity and merit of YAL is something that unfortunately comes under fire. Conners (2013) argues that the concept of "literariness" is contrived by our perceptions. To illustrate this point with his English major students, he had a colleague restructure a Charles Schulz comic strip into a poetic form, which he gives to his students without a title or author. The class analyzes its meaning and discusses it just as they would any "real" piece of literature. When he projects the image of the actual comic strip for the class they are always amazed that it is, as one student stated, "just a comic strip" (Conners, 2013, p. 72).

Unfortunately, this is how many view YAL, as "just adolescent literature," and this carries the connotation that it is not as good as what is represented in the canon. Miller (2013, 2014) maintains that this idea is transmitted by the College Board and readers of AP exams, who have become the "gatekeepers" of what is considered good literature. Often students are afraid to use a YA text to answer question 3 of the AP English Literature and Composition exam because teachers have instructed their students that essays that cite canonical texts receive higher scores. Educators must move past this perception and begin to understand and believe that YAL is literary, and can be complex, which is an issue that will be addressed in more depth shortly.

Another barrier that teachers find when wanting to teach YAL is the feeling of a need to justify teaching this type of literature. There are resources online that can help teachers not only understand but also articulate their reasons for doing so. Websites, such as for ALA, ILA (formerly IRA), and NCTE, aid in gathering information on how to justify a text choice to parents and administrators, as well as lending support on how to deal with censorship issues (Wadham and Ostenson, 2013).

CCSS and YAL

As previously stated, the CCSS exemplar lists are lacking in their inclusion of YAL titles; however, teachers should not assume that this means they should be excluded from curriculum. In *Integrating Young Adult Literature through the Common Core Standards*, Wadham and Ostenson (2013) argue that the standards actually invite teachers to determine their own lists of texts to use because the

> standards are performance based rather than prescriptive, meaning that they describe what students ought to be able to do . . . rather than what teachers ought to do. . . . It is critical to note that the CCSS does not seek to standardize anything but the measurable outcomes of student learning. (p. 16)

Once educators understand that the standards are more of an outline of what should be accomplished by the time students reach their destination (the end of a school year) rather than how to get there, they can realize that YAL aligns well with the standards. In fact, Sheehy and Clemmons claim that "the use of YAL in content area classrooms gives teachers the ability to reach more standards and, many times, cover more content with greater depth" (p. 228).

There are three aspects of the reader and the text that the CCSS requires: an increased emphasis on informational texts, text complexity, and reader independence. Wadham and Ostenson (2013) point out that the authors of the standards left out two very important requirements: the amount of reading students partake in and the issue of reading for pleasure.

Wadham and Ostenson should be commended for discussing these omissions because literacy instructors, which all educators are now called to be, should be promoting all students to become lifelong readers. The fact that adolescents can connect to YAL increases the chance that they will read more and enjoy what they are reading. This seems like a sensible solution to the problem of finding texts that will fulfill all of the requirements, including the two additional and critical points that Wadham and Ostenson added.

The next step is making sure one chooses texts with "comparable literary merit." Ostenson and Wadham (2012), Wadham and Ostenson (2013), Glaus (2014), and Miller (2014) all make valid arguments for how YAL can be considered comparable to the classics in text complexity, and they also outline how to rate books by following the CCSS's triangle of text complexity, which includes quantitative, qualitative, and reader and task dimensions.

An important thing to note is that while the reader and task dimension is the base of the triangle (see figure 1.1), which would insinuate the idea that readers' needs are important, appendix A of the CCSS only devotes 1½ paragraphs to the discussion of this dimension in contrast to the four pages allotted for the quantitative and qualitative dimensions (Wadham and Ostenson, 2013).

This difference in the amount of attention given to the reader and task dimension indicates an understanding that the reader and what is read are important, but there is a failure to articulate how critical it is on the part of the standards' authors. Perhaps it was done on purpose to give teachers more

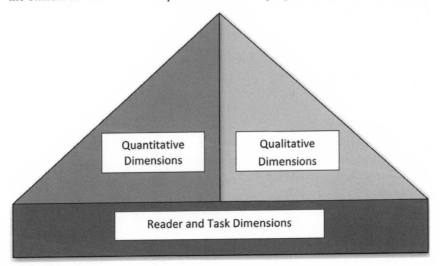

Figure 1.1.

latitude in choosing texts. Regardless, Miller (2014) concludes in his article "Text Complexity and 'Comparable Literary Merit' in Young Adult Literature" that "if a text has high text complexity, it also has 'comparable literary merit'" (p. 53); therefore, there are many YAL texts that can be used.

Merit and Research

With regard to the barrier of a lack of research in using YAL to teach content area literacy, the obvious answer is a call to more research. Much has been done and is currently being performed, but much more needs to be studied to fully understand how critical the use of YAL is in engaging students and teaching content.

Hayn, Clemmons, and Garner (2013), and Clemmons, Hayn, and Olvey (2014) have performed several studies on the use of YAL to change perceptions on social justice issues following the outline of a study done by Crag Hill using *The First Part Last* in a health class. By picking a book with a relevant and sensitive topic and administering pre- and post-reading surveys, they have found that the exposure to certain topics in the form of YAL actually changes the perceptions of pre-service teachers.

This is a simple action research methodology that any teacher-educator or classroom can use to find out whether the books s/he has chosen are truly making a difference in the thoughts of students. Topics that have been studied thus far include perceptions about second language learners, perceptions of Internet safety and whose responsibility it is to teach online safety to teens, and the theme of inclusion of all students regardless of sexual orientation, race, or socioeconomic background. Studies currently under way include topics of students' reactions to people with physical deformities, bullying, and LGBTQ issues.

The fact that YAL has its own journals is definitely helping advance research in this area. Journals such as *SIGNAL*, *JAAL*, and *The ALAN Journal* all print articles that are research-based, and *The English Journal*, which is not specific to the field of YAL, includes a number of research-based articles on this particular literature as well. At the time this chapter was being written, a new online open access journal, *Study and Scrutiny: Research in Young Adult Literature*, was being established, lending credence to the fact that more research needs to be done, as well as giving scholars and educators more avenues to publish their studies.

Similarly, Steadman, Carrol, and Froelich (2012/2013) and Bickmore and Emiraliyeva-Pitre (2012) have all worked with pre-service teachers and required them to create lesson or unit plans with YAL, and most of the pre-service teachers in these classes came to understand not only how engaging using YAL is, but also how it could be used with the standards and used successfully across content area classes. Roberts (2013) sent out e-mails to YA authors asking them to complete the following sentence: "YA literature belongs in the classroom because . . ." (p. 89).

While there were many excellent answers to the question, S. A. Bodeen answers it well by saying,

> Young adult literature belongs in the classroom because it is about the human condition known as adolescence. And young adults, who are in the utter midst of adolescent chaos, need to know that it is survivable. YA does that. (p. 89)

This condition of adolescence differs from the overall human condition in general, and Bushman and Hans (2005) make this point quite well by reminding us that

> the classics were really not intended to be read by young people at all. Even though this literature may speak to the universal human condition, young people have trouble relating because they have not experienced many of those human conditions. (p. 176)

This, of course, is one of the reasons that young adult readers have trouble connecting to the canon. They have little or no prior knowledge or experience in many of the instances to activate their schema so they can form an understanding. Bushman and Hans (2013) suggest that many adolescent readers are not cognitively ready to read many of the books being used for instruction, and educators should consider not forcing them to read these texts before they are better prepared. Clearly, helping students bridge from children's literature to adult literature is important, and YAL can serve as that bridge (Hipple, 1993; Mertz, 1993). Bushman and Hans (2013) also state,

> English professors whom we have talked to prefer incoming students who have competent writing, literary analysis, and discussion skills (all of which can be developed with quality young adult literature) instead of having a knowledge base of literature that they may or may not have understood in high school. (p. 175)

Bushman and Hans also point out that the classics make up the majority of the literary texts employed in college English courses, and suggest that college is where the classics should be taught rather than in secondary classrooms. Their argument is that if secondary teachers have done their jobs effectively, then once students get to college they will be cognitively ready to work with the different syntax many works in the canon contain. Students will be more open to reading the classics then because a connection to literature has been made, and students are ready to move on to experiencing literature that presents them with experiences and periods in time that are now not completely foreign to them.

Another reason YAL is an effective teaching tool has to do with critical thinking. The CCSS require that educators teach students how to be critical thinkers. Unfortunately these works in the canon have been overanalyzed and oftentimes have perceived "right" answers. Perceived "right" answers essentially reduce the amount of critical thinking, and in essence, negate development of what was intended (Roberts, 2013; Wolk, 2009).

Moreover, students are either told what the work means, or they research what experts have written about it, so that they are restricted from forming their own analysis or challenging others' perspectives. With YAL, educators can use inquiry methods as well as reader-response techniques to truly get the students' own opinions and thoughts, and since YAL covers topics that are relevant to today's teens, they will naturally connect the literature to their lives. Using literary theory also helps boost the argument for the literary complexity of YAL (Conners and Shepard, 2011/2012).

It is well known that not only do the CCSS demand that all teachers be responsible for literacy (CCSS, 2010; Wendt, 2013), but also the current job market requires citizens to be more literate than ever before. In the changing landscape of digital dependence, more jobs require not only literacy, but also for workers to be literate in the specific language certain positions require (Shanahan and Shanahan, 2008). This means that students must have a vast background of literacy across content areas so they will be able to effectively navigate life as productive working members of society. What better way to guide students in this skill than with the use of trade books in all classes?

There are many benefits to using YAL beyond the fact that adolescents relate better to characters and situations that are presented in it. For example, trade books enhance students' interactions with different topics, which forces them not only to use critical thinking skills, but also to form their own questions about the world around them and life in general (Alverman, Phelps, and Ridgeway, 2007; Vacca, Vacca, and Mraz, 2011). Hill (2009) states, and the authors vehemently believe this to be true,

> that integrating young adult literature in content area curriculum can raise relevant life issues through which content area teachers can address critical concepts, while also igniting the kind of authentic discussion that should be a more common experience in every classroom. (p. 29)

In his study, Hill taught *The First Part Last* to a health class to do just that. By using this text about teen pregnancy as a tool to initiate conversations and understanding about the topic, Hill was able to see perceptions changed as a result of being exposed to the book. The students were able to experience the characters' mistakes and learn from them in a safe way (Hill, 2009).

Researchers claim that there is a "mirror effect" that occurs when people connect to literature, meaning that even though the reader is not directly experiencing a character's emotions, his brain reacts as though the emotion is his own (Conners, 2014). Neuroscientists have proven that "neural networks in the mind are activated not only when people perform an action or experience an emotion, but also when they observe others perform an action or experience an emotion" (Conners, 2014, p. 35). This cognitive reaction reveals that literature has the potential to help one understand and empathize with characters, thus giving additional credence to the assertion that YAL can be an extremely effective teaching tool.

In addition to engaging adolescents to use their thinking abilities, to ask questions about the world around them, and to broaden their horizons to empathize and understand diverse people and situations different from their own, YAL can do much more. It can give teachers the ability to differentiate instruction by appropriately assigning books of different reading levels (Mertz, 1993; Vacca, Vacca, and Mraz, 2011). It can offer the same information that is given in a textbook in "a more appealing context" (Alverman, Phelps, and Ridgeway, 2007, p. 366), while at the same time moving students beyond the facts to discover more.

YAL can also help with vocabulary, even that which is content-specific, so that it will help with content area vocabulary acquisition (Alverman, Phelps, and Ridgeway, 2007). If teens connect to YAL as it is presented across content areas, they are more likely to become lifelong readers, which should be the goal of all educators, not just ELA teachers.

SUGGESTIONS FOR USING YAL IN CONTENT AREA CLASSES

Besides using a complete text for whole-class study as Hill did, how else can content area teachers utilize this wonderful resource? Book talks, which are typically used in ELA classrooms, are an effective way to get students interested in YAL that is related to a certain topic that is being studied in class. These topics can be either given by the teacher, or assigned to the students so that they are required to read something about the current topic with some freedom of choice as to which book or resource they will read.

Students tend to read what their peers recommend (Beach, Appleman, Hynds, and Wilhelm, 2011), so if a teen gives an engaging book talk it will lead to others wanting to read and explore other titles as well. This, of course, requires that teachers be knowledgeable about a range of titles on different subjects so they can suggest recommendations for texts students can choose to read for a particular assignment or unit.

Another way to garner students' interest is to employ the use of read-alouds in classes (Alverman, Phelps, and Ridgeway, 2007). While this strategy is often used in ELA classes, short read-alouds also can be used in other content area classes as discussion starters, or even to give students a different or more in-depth look at a particular topic. Alverman, Phelps, and Ridgeway (2007) state that this strategy can also be used "to introduce a new topic, to illustrate practical applications of content area concepts, and to inject a measure of humor into the classroom" (p. 371).

By using the simple method of reading aloud strategically, teachers can enhance students' understanding of and interest in a topic. Knowing that oftentimes "literature is more up-to-date than textbooks" (Alverman, Phelps, and Ridgeway, 2007, p. 366), teachers also can offer short excerpts of YAL for complementary reading to expose students to various sources related to a particular topic.

Short stories or poems are excellent ways to incorporate literature in content area classes so that students can be exposed to different types of writing, practice close reading and annotating skills, and collaborate in groups to tie the literature to the current topic as well as their own lives. Novels-in-verse have become increasingly popular, and these allow the teacher to pick and choose certain chapters to use if there is not time allotted to teach the entire book.

For example, Jacqueline Woodson's 2014 National Book Award winner, *Brown Girl Dreaming*, could be used in its entirety in an ELA or social studies class. Teachers also could focus on certain chapters to highlight specific events that are mentioned in the book that occur during the civil rights movement.

Thanhha Lai's *Inside Out and Back Again*, also a novel-in-verse, describes memories of Vietnam and tells the story of a family's journey to the United States. Again, portions of the book could be used to help ELA or social studies students understand what it is like for someone to have to move to another country for their own safety, as well as looking at the Vietnam War from a different perspective. Mathematics students could be tasked with trying to determine how far the family traveled, as well as how long it would take for one to travel using different modes of transportation. Geography and health conditions are also intertwined, so the possibilities for addressing different information across the content areas are endless.

In this chapter, the authors have established that YAL can be used to teach the standards in a more pertinent and engaging way to adolescents than by simply relying on textbooks, and they have advanced the call for all educators to teach literacy in more effective ways by using young adult literature to motivate and inform their students.

The authors firmly believe that using YAL as a tool to achieve this will benefit not only the students, but also the teachers as they work to create meaningful lessons and assessments for their classes. In the process of learning more about YAL, educators will develop a better understanding of what and how their students enjoy learning and reading, and gain a better understanding of how YAL can lead to more engagement with students as they transform into lifelong readers.

REFERENCES

Alverman, D. E., Phelps, S. F., and Ridgeway, V. G. (2007). *Content area reading and literacy: Succeeding in today's diverse classrooms.* New York, NY: Pearson.

Applebee, A. (1993). *Literature in the secondary school.* Urbana, IL: National Council of Teachers of English.

Beach, R., Appleman, D., Hynds, S., and Wilhelm, J. (2011). *Teaching literature to adolescents.* New York, NY: Routledge.

Bickmore, S. T., and Emiraliyeva-Pitre, L. (2012). Teaching diverse young adult literature in harmony with the common core state standards: Is it still just about the characters, the plot, the setting? *SIGNAL Journal, 25*(3), 20–26.

Bickmore, S. T., and Pitre, L. (2014). Moving from a novice to an expert reader/teacher of young adult literature. *The Florida English Journal, 50*(1), 37–47.

Bushman, J. H., and Hans, K. P. (2005). Young adult literature and the classics. *Using young adult literature in the English classroom* (pp. 167–85). Upper Saddle River, NJ: Pearson Education.

Clemmons, K. R., Hayn, J. A., and Olvey, H. A. (2014). Increasing awareness of cybersafety & teacher responsibility with YA lit: Action research with *Want to Go Private? Florida English Journal, 50*(1), 21–36.

Conners, S., and Shepard, I. (2011/2012). Reframing arguments for teaching YA literature in an age of common core. *SIGNAL Journal, 35*(3), 6–10.

Conners, S. P. (2013). Challenging perspectives on young adult literature. *English Journal, 102*(5), 69–73.

Conners, S. P. (2013/2014). Young adult literature: A vehicle for imagining other worlds. *SIGNAL Journal, 37*(1), 34–36.

Conners, S. P. (2014). Young adult literature: A vehicle for imagining other worlds. *SIGNAL Journal, 37*(1), 34–36.

Galda, L., and Cullinan, B. E. (1991). Literature for literacy: What research says about the benefits of using trade books in the classroom. In J. Flood, J. M. Jensen, D. Lapp, and J. R. Squire (eds.), *Handbook of research on teaching the English language arts* (pp. 529–35). New York: Macmillan.

Glaus, M. (2014). Text complexity and young adult literature: Establishing its place. *Journal of Adolescent and Adult Literacy, 57*(5), 407–16.

Hayn, J. A., Clemmons, K. R., and Garner, L. (2013). Transforming perceptions of English language learners: Action research with *Mexican Whiteboy*. *SIGNAL Journal, 36*(3), 12–14.

Hill, C. (2009). Birthing dialogue: Using *The First Part Last* in a health class. *ALAN Review, 37*(1), 29–34.

Hipple, T. (1993). Young adult literature and the test of time. In S. Sebesta and K. Donelson (eds.), *Inspiring literacy: Literature for children and young adults* (pp. 119–27). New Brunswick, NJ: Transaction Publishers.

Kittle, P. (2013). *Book love: Developing depth, stamina, and passion in adolescent readers*. Portsmouth, NH: Heinemann.

Mertz, M. P. (1993). Enhancing literary understandings through young adult fiction. In S. Sebesta and K. Donelson (eds.), *Inspiring literacy: Literature for children and young adults* (pp. 139–49). New Brunswick, NJ: Transaction Publishers.

Miller, S. J. (2013). AP gatekeeping: Exploring the myths of using YAL in an AP English classroom. *The ALAN Review, 40*(2), 79–84.

Miller, S. J. (2014). Text complexity and comparable literary merit in YAL. *The ALAN Review, 41*(2), 44–55.

National Governors Association Center for Best Practices and Council of Chief State School Officers. (2010). *Common Core State Standards for English language arts and literacy in history/social studies, science, and technical subjects*. Washington, DC: Authors.

Ostenson, J., and Wadham, R. (2012). Young adult literature and the common core: A surprisingly good fit. *American Secondary Education, 41*(1), 4–13.

Roberts, M. (2013). Teaching young adult literature: YA literature belongs in the classroom because. . . . *English Journal, 102*(5), 89–90.

Shanahan, T., and Shanahan, C. (2008). Teaching disciplinary literacy to adolescents: Rethinking content-area literacy. *Harvard Educational Review, 78*(1), 40–59.

Sheehy, C. T., and Clemmons, K. R. (2012). Beyond the language arts classroom. In J. A. Hayn and J. S. Kaplan (eds.), *Teaching young adult literature today* (pp. 225–40). Lanham, MD: Rowman & Littlefield.

Shores, J. H. (1952). The nature and scope of the problem and the attack on it: Importance, timeliness, and challenge of the conference theme. In W. S. Gray (ed.), *Improving reading in all curriculum areas: Monograph Number 76*. Chicago, IL: The University of Chicago Press.

Siebert, D., and Draper, R. J. (2008). Why content-area literacy messages do not speak to mathematics teachers: A critical content analysis. *Literacy Research and Instruction, 47*(4), 229–45.

Steadman, S. C., Carroll, P. S., and Froelich, K. S. (2011/2012). Young adult literature in Non-English/Language Arts classes? Enhancing teacher candidate and student engagement in content-area courses. *SIGNAL Journal, 35*(3), 16–19.

Stotsky, S. (2010). *FORUM 4: Literary study in grades 9, 10, and 11: A national survey*. Boston, MA: Association of Literary Scholars, Critics, and Writers.

Thomson, L. E. (2011). *Constructions of literacy: A study of reading instruction in middle school content areas*. (Doctoral dissertation). Retrieved from ERIC. (ED526370).

Vacca, R. T., Vacca, J. L., and Mraz, M. (2011). *Content area reading: Literacy and learning across the curriculum* (10th ed.). Boston, MA: Pearson.

Wadham, R. L., and Ostenson, J. W. (2013). *Integrating Young Adult Literature through the Common Core Standards.* Santa Barbara, CA: Libraries Unlimited.

Wendt, J. L. (2013). Combating the crisis in adolescent literacy: Exploring literacy in the secondary classroom. *American Secondary Education, 41*(2), 38–48.

Winsor, P. J. T. (2013). Language, literacy, and literature: Literature fair as pedagogy. *Journal of Reading Education, 38*(2), 46–52.

Wolk, S. (2009). Reading for a better world: Teaching for social responsibility with young adult literature. *Journal of Adolescent and Adult Literacy, 52*(8), 664–73.

Chapter Two

Stimulating Health Dialogue and Evaluation

Implementations of Young Adult Literature to Address Common Core Standards in Health Classes

Crag Hill and Karina R. Clemmons

In addition to the necessity to provide students with critical health content knowledge and skills, the Common Core State Standards (CCSS) adopted by forty-three states urge that "a comprehensive school-wide literacy program" include, in addition to language arts classrooms, "literacy standards in other areas such as . . . health education" (CCSS, 2010, p. 6). To this end, Common Core calls for the reading of challenging texts, both informational and literary.

New literacy expectations urge health educators to think beyond content to the literacy required to study the content—in short, to realize that in order for students to be successful in health classes, like most content classes, literacy skills are essential. Recognition that literacy is threaded throughout every textbook passage reading assignment, writing assignment, research report, and paper and pencil assessment creates a paradigm shift for educators. No longer is literacy solely the purview of elementary teachers, reading teachers, and English Language Arts teachers, as a realization emerges that almost all content classes require some form of literacy skills within the context of the discipline.

As evidenced by adoption of CCSS content literacy standards, a nationwide consensus has grown that general literacy skills are the shared responsibility of all educators. The CCSS for literacy in content areas include determining the central ideas and themes of texts, summarizing key supporting details and ideas, analyzing event and idea development, and delineating and evaluating specific claims in the text (CCSS, 2010). Today's educators are faced with accelerating expectations to integrate CCSS literacy expectations into their content classrooms, which indicate a need for more resources to help teachers with this task. This chapter is motivated by a need to contribute to varied instructional resources to support educators with new literacy benchmarks in content classes, specifically in health classes.

YAL IN HEALTH CLASSES:
A TOOL FOR LITERACY AND CONTENT

Literature has increasingly become recognized as a valuable resource beyond the English Language Arts classroom in content area classes (Austin, Thompson, and Beckman, 2006; Bean, 2002; Bean, Readence, and Baldwin, 2011; Bintz, Moore, Hayhurst, Jones, and Tuttle, 2006; Foss, 2008; Fry, 2009; Sheehy and Clemmons, 2012), and studies have supported literature's effectiveness in engaging students in content and increasing literacy skills (Bintz, 2011; Capraro and Capraro, 2006; Ellis, Taylor, and Drury, 2007; Guzzetti and Bang, 2010; Sanchez, 2007).

Contemporary young adult literature that is written, published, and marketed specifically for adolescents is a powerful resource for health educators in addition to traditional nonfiction textbooks. Through reading YAL, students are able to explore timely topics and to connect with young protagonists whose characters face similar challenges as their young readers (Featherston, 2009; Furi-Perry, 2003; Rybakova, Piotrowski, and Harper, 2013).

Fiction generally and YAL specifically have increasingly become recognized as a valuable resource beyond the English Language Arts classroom in content area classes (Austin, Thompson, and Beckman, 2006; Bean, 2002; Bean, Readence, and Baldwin, 2011; Bintz, Moore, Hayhurst, Jones, and Tuttle, 2006; Foss, 2008; Fry, 2009). Furthermore, results from studies have supported the effectiveness of fiction and YAL in engaging students in content and increasing literacy skills (Bintz, 2011; Capraro and Capraro, 2006; Ellis, Taylor, and Drury, 2007; Guzzetti and Bang, 2010; Sanchez, 2007).

The integration of YAL specifically into health classes has been suggested in order to help students engage with challenging health content (Glessner, Hoover, and Hazlett, 2006; Prater, 2000; Prater, Dyches, and Johnstun, 2006; Prater and Sileo, 2001; Sotto and Ball, 2006). Some authors have offered suggestions for how to integrate young adult and children's literature into health classes to teach tolerance of disabilities and diversity (Glessner, Hoover, and Hazlett, 2006; Prater, Dyches, and Johnstun, 2006; Sotto and Ball, 2006).

Recent studies have indicated that YAL can successfully be used to teach students in health classes about a range of topics such as the risks of teen pregnancy (Hill, 2009) and obesity ("Book Series Helps Girls Fight Obesity,"

2009), and YAL has been shown to improve literacy specifically in health classes (Deal, Jenkins, Deal, and Byra, 2010).

This chapter offers educators valuable instructional resources that seamlessly connect health standards to CCSS for literacy in content areas. Included are detailed instructional resources and examples in which YAL was integrated into high school health classes. A list of YAL titles with health themes (table 2.1) and supplemental online resources (textbox 2.1) are provided. The lessons can be used to teach the following National Health Education Standards (NHES, 2011) and Common Core State Standards for literacy in technical subjects (CCSS, 2010):

CCSS 2: Determine central ideas or themes of a text and analyze their development; summarize the key supporting details and ideas.

CCSS 3: Analyze how and why individuals, events, or ideas develop and interact over the course of a text.

CCSS 8: Delineate and evaluate the argument and specific claims in a text, including the validity of reasoning as well as the relevancy and sufficiency of evidence.

NHES 2: Students analyze the influence of family, peers, culture, media, technology, and other factors on health behavior.

NHES 4: Students demonstrate the ability to use interpersonal communication skills to enhance health and avoid or reduce health risks.

NHES 5: Students demonstrate the ability to use decision-making skills to enhance health.

RATIONALE AND IMPLEMENTATION

The compelling YAL novels *The First Part Last* (Johnson, 2004), *Staying Fat for Sarah Burns* (Crutcher, 2003), and *Wintergirls* (Anderson, 2010) have been purposefully selected for inclusion in this chapter. These YAL novels and their authors are well-respected as evidenced by multiple professional awards and inclusion in suggested teen reading lists by professional associations.

Angela Johnson's *The First Part Last* was the winner of the Young Adult Library Services Association's (YALSA) Michael L. Printz award (YALSA, 2014) and the Coretta Scott King award (American Library Association, 2014). *Staying Fat for Sarah Burns* by Chris Crutcher was awarded the California Young Reader medal ("California Young Reader Medal," 2014). Laurie Halse Anderson and Chris Crutcher were awarded YALSA's Margaret A.

Edward award for lifetime achievement for authoring significant and lasting contributions to YAL (YALSA, 2014).

The three novels in this chapter have remained popular among adolescents as evidenced by multiple reprints, as well as the novels' continued inclusion in recommended book lists from YALSA and the American Library Association. The novels include both female and male narrators, protagonists, and characters, helping make them approachable to a varied classroom audience.

The accompanying lesson plans and assessment strategies are designed to engage students in discussion and analysis of challenging health content while seamlessly integrating CCSS literacy standards. The novels enhance health content by engaging students in dialogue on a diverse range of difficult themes that are likely to be covered in a health classroom. Standards include analyzing the effect of interpersonal relationships on health behaviors, improving decision-making skills related to health, and developing strategies to improve decisions related to health.

The health themes contained within the selected YAL novels invite meaningful discussion on many profound health topics facing adolescents today (American Academy of Child and Adolescent Psychiatry, 2014). The YAL novels offer opportunities for disrupting stereotypes about teen pregnancy and teen parenting, forming foundations of healthy relationships, building resilience, understanding and managing emotions, supporting suicide prevention, managing stress and anxiety, developing a positive identity, and understanding the visceral consequences of eating disorders and other self-destructive behaviors.

For each novel, core concepts of the health curriculum are combined with CCSS and descriptions of interactive strategies such as small-group discussion with student-generated questions, role-playing, and the use of collaborative technologies such as classroom wikis or blogs. A pre-/post-test to measure student attitudes about the themes covered is included. Lesson plans integrate health standards and CCSS to prompt students to identify central ideas and themes and to analyze how the themes and ideas contribute to the health concepts being studied.

Detailed instructions for activities and assessments require students to support their findings by generating a summary of key details; to evaluate the validity of arguments and claims made in the text; to analyze how characters, plot events, themes, and ideas develop and interact over the course of the novel; and to articulate how those literary elements connect with concepts in the health curriculum. Links to additional online resources are also included (textbox 2.1).

TEXTBOX 2.1:
ADDITIONAL RESOURCES FOR IMPLEMENTATION

- Chapter discussion questions for Crutcher's *Staying Fat with Sarah Byrnes*:
  www.heinemann.com/shared/companionResources/E01032/CTM1
  .doc

- Common Core Standards for Health Made Easy: 20 Activities to Align Your Program:
  www.teacherspayteachers.com/Product/Common-Core-Standards-for
  -Health-Made-Easy-20-Activities-to-Align-Your-Program-456458

- Common Core Standards & Health Sciences Physical Education:
  www.sparkpe.org/physical-education-resources/common-core

- Discussion Questions for *Wintergirls*:
  www.bookbrowse.com/reading_guides/detail/index.cfm/book
  _number/2268/wintergirls

- Teaching Books.net Meet the Author Program: Angela Johnson, slide-shows of the author discussing her books and the writing process:
  www.teachingbooks.net/author_collection.cgi?id=28&a=1

- YAL Book Lists with Health Themes:
  www.goodreads.com/shelf/show/body-image

  www.goodreads.com/list/show/2160.YA_Drug_Substance
  _Abuse_Novels

- List of Contemporary YA Fiction Featuring Sex, Drugs, and Rock 'n' Roll (Edgy Stuff) Book List
  www.stackedbooks.org/2012/11/contemporary-ya-fiction-featuring
  -sex.html

DISCUSSING TEEN PREGNANCY AND UNPLANNED PARENTHOOD WITH *THE FIRST PART LAST*

Angela Johnson's *The First Part Last* chips away at some of the most mono-lithic stereotypes in contemporary U.S. culture: compounding irresponsible sexual activity, teens are emotionally unequipped to be parents and make many irreversible mistakes in raising their children; black males abandon the mothers of their children; males, of all ages and ethnicities, are incapable of or unwilling to contribute to the parenting of their children.

In *The First Part Last*, young African Americans Bobby and Nia have become parents of a girl, Feather. Due to complications that hospitalized Nia (readers do not find this out until late in the novel, however), Bobby is raising their child. Though Bobby, a high school senior, lives at his parents' house, his parents expect him to take full responsibility of his daughter. When Feather cries, Bobby must figure out what she needs, even if it is the middle of a school night. When she needs changing, Bobby does the changing. When Feather needs a babysitter, it is his responsibility to get her there and to pick her up. His parents offer advice and moral support, but Bobby is as much on his own as if he and his daughter were living in their own home.

The First Part Last can be a valuable part of the health curriculum, especially as the focal point of a unit on pregnancy and parenting. To fully understand the consequences of teen pregnancy, it is critical that teenagers become acutely aware of what it takes to be a parent, what the day-to-day responsibilities consist of, and what roles each of the parents have.

Standards

In this unit, students determine the central ideas and themes of *The First Part Last*, analyzing development and summarizing the key supporting details and ideas (CCSS, 2). Students analyze how and why Bobby changes over the course of the novel as a result of being a parent (CCSS, 3). With Bobby as a model, students analyze the influence of family, peers, and other factors on the health behavior of parent and child (NHES, 2).

Through a variety of interactive discussions, students develop and demonstrate the ability to use interpersonal communication skills to communicate about their health needs (NHES, 4). Using Bobby as a model, students demonstrate the ability to use decision-making skills to enhance their health and the health of the children they may be responsible for in the future (NHES, 5). The following discussion strategies are alternatives to traditional whole-class discussions, and have been successfully used with a high school health teacher (Hill, 2009).

Four-Corner Debate

To begin a substantive conversation, it is important to first unearth the students' presuppositions about teen pregnancy and parenting. As a pre-reading activity, begin with a pre-reading survey (textbox 2.2) that asks students to agree or disagree with statements such as "Teen parents are capable of taking

TEXTBOX 2.2: PRE/POST-READING
SURVEY FOR *THE FIRST PART LAST*

Directions: After reading each statement, circle the letters that best correspond to your level of agreement. SA=Strongly Agree, A=Agree, D=Disagree, SD=Strongly Disagree

1. Teen parents are capable of taking good care of a baby.
   SA / A / D / SD

2. Teen parents should continue to attend school while taking care of a baby.
   SA / A / D / SD

3. The families of teen parents should help take care of a baby.
   SA / A / D / SD

4. Teen parents do not regularly use birth control.
   SA / A / D / SD

5. Teen pregnancies are always unplanned.
   SA / A / D / SD

6. Teen mothers should give the baby up for adoption.
   SA / A / D / SD

7. It is the girl's responsibility to take care of contraception to avoid pregnancy.
   SA / A / D / SD

8. Teaching sex education helps teens avoid unplanned pregnancy.
   SA / A / D / SD

9. Teen parents are less likely to get an education and find good jobs.
   SA / A / D / SD

10. Teenagers do not have the emotional maturity or resources to parent a child.
    SA / A / D / SD

good care of a baby" or "Teen parents are less likely to complete their education and find good jobs." In Hill's (2009) study, a similar survey served as an anticipation guide and produced a snapshot of the different attitudes the male and female students in the class professed about teen parenting. For example, female students believed that teens could be fully capable of parenting while males believed they were not.

An immediate follow-up to the survey would be to organize a four-corner debate using the ten statements on the survey. For each statement, students sort themselves into one of four corners: strongly agree with the statement, agree, disagree, and strongly disagree. Allow students a few minutes to collaborate and plan to explain their rating. Call on each corner, asking students to support their positions. This helps students not only formulate their own positions, but also engage with other students and their points of view. This activity could be repeated during or after reading the novel, asking students to support their positions with evidence from the novel.

Silent Discussion

A silent discussion is an excellent strategy to get all students engaged in "talking" about the book. Halfway into the novel, have students write open-ended questions such as "What is Bobby learning about himself as he raises Feather?" "What might happen to Feather and Bobby in the future?" "In what ways has your position on teen parenting changed or been reinforced by the novel?" Then for at least fifteen minutes, circulate the sheets of paper that contain each question for students to answer in writing. Ask students not only to answer the original question, but also to write responses to the other answers.

Direct students to read the questions and answers, making sure to allow time for follow-up questions and responses. As the questions are student-generated and students have time to think, process, and write thoughtful answers, the class covers many of the prominent issues in the novel. This technique allows for a thoughtful discussion of issues that students find most relevant.

Jigsaw Discussion

Jigsaw discussions also ensure that discussions are inclusive. Instruct students to generate questions, one specific to the novel, for example, "What would you do in Bobby's place?" and one related to issues that are tangential to the novel, for example, "What are some ways society can deal with teen pregnancy?" In groups of four, have students share and discuss their questions and collaboratively decide on two questions to bring to the next round.

Form new groups of four to discuss the questions that moved forward. For closure, ask each group to report on the discussion of one of their questions. Instruct students to individually write an exit ticket that states one point they heard in the discussions that resonated as particularly important and one thing they would still like to say about a topic. The next class can begin by reading the ideas on the exit tickets and asking for further comments.

Assessment

Readminister the pre-reading survey after reading the novel, asking students not only to mark "agree" or "disagree," but also to write an explanation of their response based on the content of the novel and the class activities. Repeat the four-corner debate, adapting the survey statements to the novel, for example, "Bobby does not take care of his baby" and "Bobby's parents should help him take care of Feather." Require students to choose three of the statements and write an explanation of why they did or did not change their positions on them.

GRAPPLING WITH ABUSE, BODY IMAGE, AND RESILIENCY WITH *STAYING FAT FOR SARAH BYRNES*

Close friendships often encompass an explicitly stated commitment to "be there" for the other, especially at life's most difficult points. Chris Crutcher's *Staying Fat for Sarah Byrnes* enacts just such a commitment. Eric Calhoune, aka Moby, because of his above-average girth, has been Sarah Byrnes's loyal friend since the eighth grade. Sarah, scarred by serious burns to her face and upper body, pushes everyone else away, fiercely protecting her private space.

Both Moby and Sarah, with wits sharpened in response to years of bullying, have found ways to live outside the school's mainstream and to fight back at bullies, peer and adult alike. But when Sarah is hospitalized in a catatonic state, Moby redoubles his efforts to reach out to her and help her, and as a result of these efforts also becomes a spokesman for others who are bullied, including those he may not know well. Stand up for others, *Staying Fat for Sarah Byrnes* declares, but more importantly, at the same time stand up for yourself.

Staying Fat for Sarah Byrnes is filled with health content topics relevant to adolescent readers. Themes include building healthy relationships, developing effective interpersonal communication, resolving conflicts with peers and parents, responding to peer pressure, protecting oneself from violence and abuse, and becoming an advocate for oneself and others. Through Moby and Sarah's example—embodied fictional experiences we hope our students do not have to endure (fully aware that many do)—students can engage concepts, language, and self-awareness, to help them navigate their personal and social worlds on their own terms.

Standards

In this unit with *Staying Fat for Sarah Byrnes*, students analyze how and why Moby, Sarah, and other characters, major plot events, and health concepts develop and interact over the course of the novel (CCSS, 3). Students analyze the influence of family, peers, culture, and other factors on the health behavior of the characters, while considering how these factors play out in their own lives (NHES, 2).

Using Moby, Sarah, and other characters as models, students demonstrate the ability to use interpersonal communication skills to enhance their health and avoid or reduce their health risks (NHES, 4). Using Moby, Sarah, and other characters as examples, students demonstrate the ability to use decision-making skills to enhance their health (NHES, 5). The following strategies can be used to enhance important health curriculum concepts while at the same time addressing literacy standards. Developed in collaboration with a health teacher, these strategies have all been successively used in a high school health class.

Social Mobile

By the time Moby gets to his senior year, he has developed a solid support system: his friend and teammate Ellerby; his swim coach and English teacher, Ms. Lemry; and his mother. Sarah, however, has not added any friends since junior high school, choosing instead to withdraw from everything and everyone, including Moby. Early in the study of the novel, to help students understand the important qualities of a friendship and to help them identify their support systems, ask them to create a social mobile for themselves.

Materials needed:
White index cards
Paper clips
Pens
Colored paper

Procedure to create a social mobile:

1. Write your name on the front of an index card. On the back of the card, identify and write down five qualities that you believe are important for friends to possess. Pick one color of paper and cut 5 squares about half the size of the index card. On each square write one quality from this list.
2. Next, list the people in your life who fit these qualities. Include people of all ages. Count the number of people who are eighteen years of age and older. These are caring adults in your life. Choose a different color of paper and cut a circle for each of these people and write one name per circle.
3. Count the number of people seventeen years of age and younger. Choose a different color and cut a triangle for each of these people and write one name per triangle.
4. Assemble the mobile with paper clips by hooking squares below the index card, and hooking circles and triangles to the squares. Hang the mobiles in the classroom.

As students continue reading the novel, talk about the support system—or lack thereof—of the characters, considering how their lives might be different with an interpersonal support system in place.

Cross the Line

Bullying is a theme present in *Staying Fat for Sarah Byrnes*, sometimes in the foreground and sometimes in the background. Both Moby and Sarah were bullied in junior high by their peers and, arguably, by an administrator. One of the minor characters, Jody, is bullied by her boyfriend, Mark, who it can be argued is also being bullied by Moby and Ellerby in class and at swim practice. This novel shows that bullying can be sometimes overt and other times subtle, and can be something we all may have done unwittingly. The activity "Cross the Line" makes that explicit.

Instruct students to line up in two lines facing each other or, if there is space, in a square so that everyone is in view. Start slowly to show that we all have many things in common in a school setting by stating "Cross the line if you have ever forgotten to do your homework" or "Cross the line if you have trouble getting out of bed to go to school." Then begin to insert more serious statements such as "Cross the line if you or someone you know has ever been bullied." "Cross the line if you or someone you know has ever bullied anyone." "Cross the line if you or someone you know has observed someone being bullied." Twenty-five to thirty statements are sufficient.

Through this activity, students see that, like Moby and Sarah, few remain untouched by bullying in some way. A follow-up discussion should debrief what students observed and should brainstorm ways to deal with bullying as individuals and as a school community.

Developmental Assets

In the novel, Moby and Sarah, despite Moby's efforts, have grown apart. As Moby pursues athletics and begins to think about his future, Sarah remains static, trying to cope with the stresses in her life by withdrawing. Not even Moby is privy to what is causing Sarah so much pain. Building on the social mobile activity, the following activity engages students in drawing a contrast between the two characters.

Direct students to complete the "40 Developmental Assets for Adolescents" survey online at www.search-institute.org/content/40-developmental -assets-adolescents-ages-12-18 (Search Institute, 2014) from the perspective of one of the characters. Students find that Moby has acquired more than a dozen internal and external assets such as "Family provides high levels of love and support" and "Young person places high value on promoting equality and reducing hunger and poverty." Sarah, however, has acquired but a handful of these assets, for example, "Young person acts on convictions and stands up for her beliefs." A follow-up discussion should focus on ways that Sarah can acquire more of these assets, both external and internal, so that she can increase her agency.

Assessment

Students should develop an action plan in which they outline a plan for identifying stressors in their relationships, in their schools, and in the larger community; for creating and sustaining healthy relationships; and for making healthy decisions. The action plan should include not only a description of actions the students themselves may take, but also a list of how other people would be involved and include a timetable to put this plan into action.

STRUGGLING WITH GRIEF, EATING DISORDERS, AND SELF-MUTILATION WITH *WINTERGIRLS*

Adolescents experience persistent, virtually daily pressure related to body image, sexuality, and relationships with friends and family members as they progress toward an as-yet-undefined future. Now that it is commonplace for many teenagers to have cell phones, adolescents are less likely to gain any respite from these pressures. Adolescents have less and less time, it seems, to sort things out for themselves in their own time and space. When adolescents find themselves in difficult places, they may not possess the developmental assets to help them extricate themselves.

A unit utilizing Laurie Halse Anderson's *Wintergirls* as the springboard for learning about healthy and risky health behaviors can be a useful, relevant course of study. It is important when initiating a discussion on eating disorders, however, that teachers keep in mind that while weight and body image are important issues to students, it is more important to focus instructional time on healthy lifestyles rather than on the eating disorders themselves. Through studying *Wintergirls*, students confront the grim realities the main character faces as the result of a series of risky decisions. The instructional strategies included here also engage students in the issues the novel raises, as well as asking students to focus on healthy lifestyle choices.

Wintergirls tackles difficult topics through the experiences of the teenaged narrator, Lia. Lia and her best friend, Cassie, have indeed backed themselves into a corner, competing with each other to see which of the two can lose the most weight, all the while ignoring the advice and desperate actions from their families. Rather than lean on each other to build positive identities, Lia and Cassie pull each other down.

Wintergirls opens with Cassie's death, and Lia's trajectory tumbles downhill from there. Rather than change her behavior, a destructive lifestyle of weight loss and deceit she shared with Cassie, Lia continues to distance herself from her family. Unable to deal with her grief and unwilling to seek out counseling, Lia attempts to remain in control by placing obstacles between herself and others, such as lying and not accepting help when offered. As a result, Lia loses touch with reality, ultimately collapsing at the motel where Cassie died alone. Having hit bottom, Lia finally confronts her biggest regret and begins the long healing process.

Standards

In this unit with *Wintergirls* as a centerpiece, students identify the central ideas of the novel, such as the consequences of risky behaviors, and analyze how these ideas contribute to Lia's development, identifying key scenes for supporting evidence (CCSS, 2). Students analyze how and why Lia's health is affected by her destructive relationship with Cassie and her response to Cassie's death over the course of the novel (CCSS, 3). At the end of the novel, students delineate and evaluate the argument the author makes about eating disorders, identify specific claims the novel makes, and debate the validity of reasoning as well as the relevancy and sufficiency of evidence for these claims (CCSS, 8).

Students analyze the influence of family, peers, culture, and other positive and negative factors on Lia and Cassie's health behavior (NHES, 2). To help students prepare for experiences with grief and other traumatic events, instructional activities call on students to demonstrate the ability to use interpersonal communication skills to enhance health and avoid or reduce health risks (NHES, 4). With Lia and Cassie as negative models, students demonstrate the ability to use decision-making skills to enhance health (NHES, 5).

The Power of Body Image

To alert students to how society impacts body image and self-esteem, the following Body Image Poster activity asks them to evaluate images in print and digital media for positive and negative depictions of body image.

Materials:
Images printed from computer and selected from print magazines
Scissors
Glue sticks
Poster board

As a class, brainstorm a list of positive and negative images commonly found in media; then have students individually search the Internet and/or peruse print magazines for examples of these positive and negative images. Students should create a compare/contrast poster that counters the negative body images students have encountered in the media with concepts of positive self-identity. The poster should include explanations for why an image is positive or negative. For closure, ask students to write a brief argument for why their poster should be published online or in a print magazine in place of the negative ads. This activity can also be created, shared, and published on a classroom wiki using a site such as www.pbworks.com.

In the follow-up "What's Television Promoting?" activity, instruct students to take notes while watching television for at least two hours over the course of a week, listing examples of programs and/or commercials that promote healthy body images. As an extension of this critical viewing, ask students to write, peer-proofread and edit, and mail a letter to television stations or product lines thanking them for their ads or shows promoting healthy body images and lifestyles.

Research Groups

To combat the many myths about eating disorders before reading *Wintergirls*, ask students to compile a list of the physical, psychological, and social effects of eating disorders and, more importantly, list how they know about these effects (e.g., media, personal experience, health class, etc.). Divide the class into three research groups.

Group 1 should research the physical effects of eating disorders, and then track the physical effects of Lia and Cassie's eating disorders throughout the novel, noting when these effects are accurately and/or inaccurately portrayed.

Group 2 should research the psychological effects of eating disorders, and then track Lia and Cassie's psychological behaviors through the novel, measuring accuracy of depiction against their research.

Group 3 should research the social effects of eating disorders, such as how an eating disorder impacts not only an individual's social life, but also the lives of family members and friends. Students can then review the events in the novel to track how Lia and Cassie's behavior affects the lives of their friends and family members. Each group should report on their findings to initiate a culminating class discussion.

Online Discussion

Throughout the novel, ask students to contribute to an online discussion board on the novel twice per week, with one original post and one response to a classmate's post. Discussion topics could include the following: substantive commentary on the novel; reflections on healthfulness of personal food consumption and subsequent energy level; observations of the health decisions Lia has been making or avoiding paired with possible solutions; consideration of Lia's grief and healthier options for her to process grief.

Assessment

Organize students into groups of two to three to create skits in which they role-play scenes from the novel. Rather than play out the negative scenarios as they occurred in the novel, ask students to show how these situations could have been handled in healthier ways. For example, instead of keeping her grief to herself, what could Lia have done differently? How could she have let people know she feels she let Cassie down by not answering her calls the night she died? How could she have talked to her stepmother? How could she have approached a peer or a teacher at school?

STIMULATING HEALTHY DIALOGUE AND CONTENT LITERACY WITH YAL

CCSS for literacy call for the integration of nonfiction and fiction texts in all content areas (CCSS, 2010). YAL complements nonfiction informational texts frequently used in health classes to convey information on varied health topics in a way that is accessible and engaging to adolescents. Reading the selected YAL novels and engaging students in active discussion, critical thinking, and problem-solving related to the topics offers health educators another angle to approach health themes. Rather than a third-person explication of complex health risks, YAL offers students a more intimate perspective as they read the personal experiences of young characters faced with difficult challenges.

Health literacy is inextricably tied with other literacies. Grounded in current classroom research, this chapter demonstrates the power of YAL to engage students in a dialogue on essential health themes and offers educators vital resources to cover CCSS for literacy while enhancing health content (table 2.1). YAL informs students with diverse peer perspectives on contemporary health issues and empowers health teachers with relevant resources to engage challenging health topics and literacy.

Table 2.1. Additional YAL Titles with Health Themes

Title	Author	Year	Topics/Issues
Bad Apple	Laura Ruby	2009	cyberbullying
Beneath a Meth Moon	Jacqueline Woodson	2012	substance abuse
Boost	Kathy Mackel	2008	unhealthy dieting, diet aids, steroids, pressure of competitive sports
By the Time You Read This, I'll Be Dead	Julie Anne Peters	2011	"suicide completer" websites, blogging community
Clean	Amy Reed	2011	drug addiction, rehabilitation
Deadline	Chris Crutcher	2009	living life after terminal diagnosis
Freaks Like Us	Susan Vaught	2012	mental illness, schizophrenia
Gym Candy	Carl Deuker	2008	steroid use

continued

Table 2.1. Continued

Title	Author	Year	Topics/Issues
Hate List	Jennifer Brown	2010	bullying, post-traumatic stress, guilt and blame
Identical	Ellen Hopkins	2008	drug and alcohol abuse, sexual molestation, self-destructive behavior
I Will Save You	Matt de la Peña	2011	mental illness, psychological trauma
Life in the Fat Lane	Cherie Bennett	2011	metabolic syndrome, body image
Scars	Cheryl Rainfield	2010	sexual abuse, cutting
Skinny	Donna Cooner	2014	obesity, gastric bypass surgery, body image
The Fault in Our Stars	John Green	2012	living with cancer
The Fold	An Na	2008	body image, plastic surgery to alter Asian eyes
The Impossible Knife of Memory	Laurie Halse Anderson	2014	caretaking parent with post-traumatic stress syndrome
Thirteen Reasons Why	Jay Asher	2011	suicide, consequences of decisions, rape
Tricks	Ellen Hopkins	2011	depression, prostitution
Tweetheart	Elizabeth Rudnick	2010	misrepresentation in online identity
Unfriended	Rachel Vail	2014	cyberbullying, flaming
Unfriended: A Top 8 Novel	Kate Finn	2011	cyberbullying
Want to Go Private?	Sarah Littman	2013	inadvertent involvement with Internet child predator
Willow	Julia Hoban	2009	dealing with tragedy, cutting
Zitface	Emily Howse	2011	severe acne, body image

REFERENCES

American Academy of Child and Adolescent Psychiatry. (2014). Facts for families. Retrieved from www.aacap.org/AACAP/Families_and_Youth/Facts_for_Families/Facts_for_Families_Keyword.aspx.

American Library Association. (2014). Coretta Scott King book award recipients. Retrieved from www.ala.org/emiert/cskbookawards/recipients.

Anderson, L. H. (2010). *Wintergirls*. New York, NY: Speak.

Austin, R., Thompson, D., and Beckman, E. (2006). Locusts for lunch: Connecting mathematics, science, and literature. *Mathematics Teaching in the Middle School, 12*(4), 182–87.

Bean, T. W. (2002). Making reading relevant for adolescents. *Educational Leadership, 60*(3), 34–37.

Bean, T. W., Readence, J., and Baldwin, R. S. (2011). *Content area literacy: An integrated approach* (10th ed.). Dubuque, IA: Kendall Hunt.

Bintz, W. P. (2011). "Way-In" books encourage exploration in middle grades classrooms. *Middle School Journal, 42*(3), 34–45.

Bintz, W. P., Moore, S. D., Hayhurst, E., Jones, R., and Tuttle, S. (2006). Integrating literacy, math, and science to make learning come alive. *Middle School Journal, 37*(3), 30–7.

Book series helps girls fight obesity. (2009). *Curriculum Review, 48*(5), 7–8.

California Young Reader Medal. (2014). California Young Reader Medal winners. Retrieved from http://californiayoungreadermedal.org/winners.htm#32007.

Capraro, R. M., and Capraro, M. M. (2006). Are you really going to read us a story? Learning geometry through children's mathematics literature. *Reading Psychology, 27,* 21–36.

Common Core State Standards (CCSS). (2010). Common core state standards for English language arts and literacy in history/social studies, science, and technical subjects. Retrieved from www.corestandards.org/the-standards.

Crutcher, C. (2003). *Staying fat for Sarah Byrnes.* New York, NY: Greenwillow.

Deal, T. B., Jenkins, J. M., Deal, L. O., and Byra, A. (2010). The impact of professional development to infuse health and reading in elementary schools. *American Journal of Health Education, 41*(3), 155–66.

Ellis, R., Taylor, C., and Drury, H. (2007). Learning science through writing: Association with prior conceptions of writing and perceptions of a writing program. *Higher Education, Research & Development, 26*(3), 297–311.

Featherston, K. (2009). The transforming power of young adult literature. *The ALAN Review, 37*(1), 7–11.

Foss, S. M. (2008). Literature in the mathematics classroom: Introducing *The Inch Boy* to middle school students. *Mathematics Teaching in the Middle School, 13*(9), 538–42.

Fry, S. W. (2009). Exploring Social Studies through multicultural literature: *Legend of the St. Ann's flood. Social Studies, 100*(2), 85–92.

Furi-Perry, U. (2003). "Dude, that book was cool": The reading habits of young adults. *Reading Today, 20*(2), 24–25.

Glessner, M. M., Hoover, J. H., and Hazlett, L. A. (2006). The portrayal of overweight in adolescent fiction. *Reclaiming Children and Youth, 15*(2), 116–23.

Guzzetti, B., and Bang, E. (2010). The influence of literacy-based science instruction on adolescents' interest, participation, and achievement in science. *Literacy, Research and Instruction, 50*(1), 44–67.

Hill, C. (2009). Birthing dialogue: Using *The First Part Last* in a health class. *ALAN Review, 37*(1), 29–34.

Johnson, A. (2004). *The first part last.* New York, NY: Simon Pulse.

National Health Education Standards (NHES). (2011). Retrieved from www.cdc.gov/ healthyyouth/sher/standards/index.htm.

Prater, M. A. (2000). Using juvenile literature with portrayals of disabilities in your classroom. *Intervention in School and Clinic, 35*(3), 167–76.

Prater, M. A., Dyches, T. T., and Johnstun, M. (2006). Teaching students about learning disabilities through children's literature. *Intervention in School and Clinic, 42*(1), 14–24.

Prater, M. A., and Sileo, N. M. (2001). Using juvenile literature about HIV/AIDS: Ideas and precautions for the classroom. *Teaching Exceptional Children, 33*(6), 34–45.

Rybakova, K., Piotrowski, A., and Harper, E. (2013). Teaching controversial young adult literature with the Common Core. *Wisconsin English Journal, 55*(1), 37–45.

Sanchez, R. (2007). Music and poetry as social justice texts in the secondary classroom. *Theory and Research in Social Education, 35*(4), 646–66.

Search Institute. (2014). 40 developmental assets for adolescents survey. Retrieved from www.search-institute.org/content/40-developmental-assets-adolescents-ages -12-18.

Sheehy, C., and Clemmons, K. R. (2012). Beyond the language arts classroom: The dynamic intersection of young adult literature and technological, pedagogical, and content knowledge. In J. Hayn and J. Kaplan (eds.), *Teaching young adult literature today: Insights, considerations, and perspectives for the classroom teacher.* New York, NY: Taylor and Francis.

Sotto, C. D., and Ball, A. L. (2006). Dynamic characters with communication disorders in children's literature. *Intervention in School and Clinic, 42*(1), 40–45.

Young Adult Library Services Association (YALSA). (2014). YALSA book awards. Retrieved from www.ala.org/yalsa/booklistsawards/bookawards.

Chapter Three

Knowing Readers and Knowing Books

Using Text Complexity Measures to Select Texts and Motivate Adolescent Readers

Linda T. Parsons and Patricia E. Bandré

The tenth anchor standard of the Common Core State Standards for English Language Arts expects students to "read and comprehend complex literary and informational texts independently and proficiently" (www.corestandards .org/ELA-Literacy/CCRA/R). Few administrators, teachers, or parents question the need for students to read and comprehend a variety of texts with a high level of independence and proficiency; however, the need for this text to be complex has resulted in many people asking, "What is complex text?" To answer this question, the standards suggest the use of a three-part model that includes qualitative dimensions, includes quantitative dimensions, and takes the reader and the task into consideration.

The graphic representation of these three dimensions, an isosceles triangle divided into three identical pieces, visually demonstrates the intention for these three areas to receive equal consideration. Qualitative aspects include the levels of meaning within the text, the way the text is structured, the language used in the text, and the level of prior knowledge the reader possesses relating to the content of the text. Professional judgment is necessary to assess each of these areas.

Computer software, on the other hand, easily assesses the quantitative elements of text, which include sentence length, word length, word frequency, and text cohesion. Often referred to as readability, quantitative measures of complexity include the Fry Graph, Lexiles, and the Dale-Chall Readability Formula, among others, the first of which was published in 1923 (Fry, 2002). Reader and task considerations, the final measure, cannot be assessed by a computer and require careful professional consideration of the reader's cognitive capabilities, level of motivation, and amount of background knowledge.

Additionally, the purpose for reading the text and the outcome desired warrant consideration. While tools for measuring these three facets of complexity exist, they are "at once useful and imperfect. Each . . . has its limitations and none is completely perfect" (appendix A, p. 8). Consequently, matching readers to text is one of the most difficult and important tasks teachers do each day. "Making the match between book and reader relies on knowledge in three areas: knowing the reader, knowing the book, and knowing the technique for bringing book and reader together" (Lesesne, 2003, p. 1). Students need to read widely and deeply, and they need plenty of experience with complex texts—"texts that offer them new language, new knowledge, and new modes of thought" (Adams, 2009).

KNOWING THE READER

Knowing the reading preferences and habits of adolescents is essential when selecting complex texts for the classroom. Studies in the field of adolescent literature delineate a number of characteristics reported by young adults as important when selecting books. Using the Adolescent Motivation to Read Profile (AMRP), Pitcher et al. (2007) interviewed middle school students about their reading preferences and their motivation to read. Findings demonstrated the importance of choice; students' frequent use of multi-literacies, including print sources such as magazines and newspapers as well as electronic sources like e-mail, text messages, and instant messages; and the influence of family, friends, and teachers on their reading habits. In addition, students who participated in the study noted their need to feel connected to the topic of the text.

Middle school students participating in a study conducted by Kelley, Wilson, and Koss (2012) also noted the influence of personal connections to content on their motivation to read. Participants reported being influenced by the author and genre of a book as well as their level of background knowledge about the topic. When surveyed and interviewed, students reported a preference of realistic fiction, fantasy/science fiction, and mystery over other genres. Students wanted to be hooked by the book from the very beginning of the story, and they desired to read books with characters close to their own age—characters whose actions were relatable and who realistically portrayed the identity issues with which adolescents grapple.

Recent inquiries conducted by Miller and Kelley (2014) reinforce the gravitation of students toward texts depicting the peaks and valleys of adolescence. Many of the students they questioned listed realistic fiction as a favorite genre. One student reported, "I like realistic fiction because I can relate to the situations, and sometimes if it is the right book, I can actually get some tips for what I'm going through because the character is going through the same situation" (p. 167). This student's comment echoes the sentiments of Atwell (2007), who iterates the value of students using text to make sense of their world.

Personal connections with text influence reader motivation, and reader motivation paired with cognitive competence influences engagement (Guthrie and Davis, 2003). According to Schussler (2009), engagement results when students develop an interest in and form a "deeper connection" with text (p. 115).

Text Complexity: Reader and Task Considerations

The Common Core State Standards for English Language Arts (2010) stress the importance of student engagement as it pertains to text complexity. The Standards require teachers and students to dig deeper and go beyond making meaning in order to reach greater levels of understanding. The Standards expect reader engagement. Knowing the reader and considering the task are essential when measuring text complexity. The Standards document reminds us that "such factors as students' motivation, knowledge and experiences must also come into play in text selection.

"Students deeply interested in a given topic, for example, may engage with texts on that subject across a range of complexity. Particular tasks may also require students to read harder texts than they would normally be required to" (p. 9). Teachers must select texts that spark conversation, encourage students to consider diverse viewpoints, and align to the outcome of the task. Text selection must be intentional (Moley, Bandré, and George, 2011).

Content area teachers can use the research on adolescent reading preferences and motivation when selecting complex texts to support and extend concepts taught in their classes. While nonfiction texts are inherent to the teaching of content area topics, literature can help students reach a greater "depth of conceptual development" (Hancock, 2008, p. 381). "It is crucial [for teachers] to realize that all genres of literature can contribute to conceptual understanding" (p. 380).

Carefully chosen pieces of literature focused on a specific topic provide readers with a variety of perspectives. Through these texts, readers encounter new vocabulary, build their knowledge about the topic, and compare and contrast the viewpoints presented: actions prompted by complex texts. Two recently published, award-winning works of young adult fiction, *Maggot*

Moon (Gardner, 2013) and *Code Name Verity* (Wein, 2012) illustrate this point. Each book provides multiple perspectives on war and the implications of war, topics commonly addressed in secondary social studies classrooms. Reader and task considerations must be taken into account when determining the complexity of these two books.

Maggot Moon

In this book, Standish Treadwell, age 15, narrates an alternative history wherein Gardner imagines a country resembling Nazi Germany as the victor of a world war. Considered impure by the totalitarian Motherland, Standish is consigned to live in Zone 7, where life is a brutal mix of extreme poverty, frequent hunger, and indiscriminate abuse and surveillance. Standish's parents have disappeared, and his best friend, Hector, and his parents are taken after Hector discovers the Motherland's secret. When the Moon Man appears, Standish and his grandfather hide him and learn the secret as well; the Motherland is planning to fabricate a moon landing to establish worldwide control through the threat of weaponry aimed at the earth. Like David against Goliath, Standish risks everything to expose the Motherland's deception.

Readers will approach *Maggot Moon* in unique ways dependent upon their cognitive capabilities, background knowledge, motivation, and specific task demands. To successfully comprehend this text, a reader needs to be able and willing to "postpone clarity" (Barnhouse and Vinton, 2012, p. 49) and "tolerate a fair amount of uncertainty" (p. 162). Readers of *Maggot Moon* must be flexible in their thinking: willing to entertain multiple possibilities and comfortable with revising inaccurate predictions. These attributes would facilitate following the complex organization of this text as time spirals back and forth, but ever forward. A reader of *Maggot Moon* must also be motivated enough to engage in a close reading to catch the many nuances within this novel.

A certain body of historical and cultural knowledge would enhance the reading of *Maggot Moon*. Knowledge of Nazi Germany is necessary for the reader to move from a surface-level reading to a deeper allegorical or metaphorical understanding, and a cursory familiarity with 1950s American television and film would aid readers in fully understanding Standish's fascination with and dream of living in the land of "Croca-Colas." Finally, a level of comfort with word usage particular to England would clear up possible confusion. Too much front-loading, however, or interrupting the flow of the story to provide background information, could lead to over-teaching the novel and dampening student motivation to simply sink into the book (Gallagher, 2009).

Offering this novel as a choice, preferably a literature circle choice, would be an ideal task demand for *Maggot Moon*. Reading this after studying the Holocaust in social studies may aid readers' engagement. The simple act of choosing increases intrinsic motivation to read (Guthrie and Humenick, 2004), and motivation is essential if readers are to engage in the kind of close reading this novel demands. Reading this novel with a group of interested peers would give students the opportunity to engage in exploratory talk (Cazden, 2001) during which they could work through their evolving understandings. The novel's complex analogies and metaphors demand more than an independent reading if students are to develop a deep understanding.

Code Name Verity

Code Name Verity opens with Queenie, a Scottish spy captured by the Gestapo, writing everything she knows about the British war effort in exchange for a reprieve from torture and a few more days of life. Within her confession, she inserts details of the suffering she endures in prison and tells of her fierce friendship with Maddie, the pilot who flew her into France. Queenie is variously known as Eva, Katharina, Verity, or Julie depending upon her current identity and role.

Meanwhile, Maddie has crash-landed the plane and was saved by the Resistance. In the final third of the book, Maddie picks up the narration and tells her side of the story and of efforts to rescue Queenie from the Gestapo. This is a story of personal friendship first and political intrigue second with subtle clues leading to a heartbreaking climax and a masterfully executed plot twist.

In many discussions of text complexity, there is no "mention of the complexity inherent in *how* they're written" (Barnhouse and Vinton, 2012, p. 47), and this complexity is enhanced when Wein purposefully misleads the reader to create tension and intrigue. We begin a text by reading "closely, looking for those textual clues that might let us know who the characters are, what seems to be happening, and when and where they are, in order to get a foothold on the story and orient ourselves" (Barnhouse and Vinton, 2012, pp. 55–56).

A reader of *Code Name Verity* must be willing and able to revise everything that has become "known" when the plot twist comes with the change of narrator. An ideal reader would also be able to "read forward while thinking backward" (Barnhouse and Vinton, 2012, p. 114) to identify the foreshadowing that supports and validates the climax of the story. Without recognition of the foreshadowing, the climax may seem unbelievable.

Readers who seek out historical fiction in general or of this time period, or those interested in aviation may be particularly motivated to read this novel.

A cursory knowledge of England's involvement in WWII and the occupation of France would prove beneficial. Additionally, knowledge of some of the literature referenced would also deepen the reader's understanding, but again, providing too much front-loading or interrupting the flow of the story to provide background information dampens student motivation to simply read and enjoy the book (Gallagher, 2009).

As with *Maggot Moon*, offering *Code Name Verity* as a literature circle choice, perhaps after studying WWII, would be an ideal task demand. Reading this novel in a group of similarly motivated peers would give students the opportunity to work through their initial understandings and later justify the reliable and unreliable narrations. Students could support each other in their understandings of vocabulary, cultural references, and the historical background. Fisher, Frey, and Lapp (2012) recommend "the academic discourse of learners as they discuss, clarify, question, provide evidence, disagree, and develop solutions" (p. 89), and the complexity of *Code Name Verity* justifies this type of accountable talk.

KNOWING THE BOOK

While knowing the reader and considering the task are essential to determining text complexity, teachers must also know a book rates qualitatively and quantitatively. Like reader and task considerations, a knowledgeable human reader must evaluate the qualitative aspects of a text. According to the Common Core State Standards for English Language Arts (2010), qualitative dimensions of text include aspects "such as levels of meaning or purpose; structure; language conventionality and clarity; and knowledge demands" (p. 4).

Quantitative aspects of text include those "such as word length or frequency, sentence length, and text cohesion, that are difficult if not impossible for a human reader to evaluate efficiently, especially in long texts, and are thus today typically measured by computer software" (p. 4).

Text Complexity: Qualitative Factors and Quantitative Factors

The level of complexity attributed to the qualitative dimensions of a text can be similar to that of the quantitative dimensions, or the two can be very different from one another. For example, a book containing simple sentences and straightforward language (quantitative aspects) may have difficult structures and require great amounts of background knowledge (qualitative aspects). Analyzing the qualitative and quantitative dimensions of *Maggot Moon* and

Code Name Verity provides an opportunity to see how the qualitative and quantitative dimensions of a text combine with the reader and task considerations to determine overall text complexity.

Maggot Moon

Maggot Moon has a Lexile Measure of 690L (Lexile, Metametrics, Inc.) based on sentence length and relative word frequency. Quantitatively, the text appears appropriate for a proficient second or third grade student. A cursory glance at the novel might support this measure. The chapters vary in length from a single page to three pages, and the amount of white space reflects that typically found in early chapter books. Qualitative factors contradict the quantitative evaluation of this book. The complexity of *Maggot Moon* lies in its organization, narration, setting, and vocabulary. This text requires the reader to go beyond surface comprehension to a deeper historical, allegorical, and metaphorical understanding.

Organization

Maggot Moon features repeated shifts in time and layers story lines rather than presenting a chronological narrative. The actual time frame of *Maggot Moon* seems to span four days, yet Standish takes us back in time to fill in the past so we can understand the present. This requires readers to "postpone clarity" (Barnhouse and Vinton, 2012, p. 49) and read in a state of "not knowing" (p. 56) for an extended length of time. Numerous flashbacks are present, sometimes occurring mid-chapter, and are subtly signaled with time references: "last winter" (p. 48), "only three weeks ago" (p. 59), "on my birthday in March, after the terrible winter" (p. 119).

Many characters are introduced early in the novel, but their role is not revealed until much later. For example, Standish mentions Hector on page 4, and on page 5 says that he disappeared, yet he is not introduced fully until pages 38–39, and he is taken away on pages 145–46. Standish mentions that his mother and father are gone on page 23, yet their disappearance is not explained until pages 120–21. Mentioning characters and withholding information about them increases the complexity of this text, forcing readers to repeatedly "draft and revise their way from confusion into eventual clarity" (Barnhouse and Vinton, 2012, p. 58).

Narration

As the narrator, Standish seems to withhold information. It is not as if we become aware as he does, but it seems he reveals information when he is ready to do so. This is evident in the organization of his narrative and in the reveal of the Motherland's hoax. Standish first realizes something is amiss when he recognizes Hector's father in the control room during the launch knowing he is, in fact, at home (p. 93). Standish admits he knows what is going on (p. 115), says he "knew then what was going on behind the wall in the garden" (p. 189), yet he does not tell the reader what is going on until page 196. This level of complexity keeps the reader "not knowing" and wondering if Standish is to be trusted.

For the first 207 pages, Standish tells the story in the past tense, yet he switches to present tense when he begins to put his plan into action. Why this switch in verb tense? After infiltrating the Motherland's film set, Standish is thrown into a cell and discovers Hector, who has been tortured so his father will cooperate with the Motherland. As we infer Hector is dying, Standish says, "I know what Hector is doing. He's escaping from here as fast as he can" (p. 261).

Later, when Standish is about to expose the hoax, Hector appears beside him and says, "We will do this together like we always did" (p. 271). Amid machine gun fire, Hector leads Standish out of the building and they drive away in "a huge, ice-cream-colored Cadillac" (p. 278) to the land of "Croca-Colas" (p. 279). Standish presents this as real, and the reader must infer that he is seeing Hector's ghost. Readers must also infer what happens to Standish when Hector pulls him to his feet on page 278. Readers might question to whom and even how Standish is narrating his story.

Setting

The setting of *Maggot Moon* is ambiguous. Readers must use historical knowledge and pay close attention to detail to situate the novel in time and place. "What is most invisible, i.e., the places that require a reader to infer" (Barnhouse and Vinton, 2012, p. 69), contribute to the complexity of a text. On the surface, we know the story takes place in Zone 7, an area controlled by the Motherland, but the deeper implications of the setting are established through inference. One specific piece of information Gardner provides readers is that "it is Thursday, nineteenth July, nineteen fifty-six" (p. 56). Beyond this, many references to Nazi Germany are visible to readers familiar with the history of that period.

For example, the reader learns that "not all from the Motherland agree with what's being done in her name" (p. 44). Hector's family has been forced to live in Zone 7 because his father refused to work on the moon project once he realized it was a hoax, and Hector's mother, a physician, refused to eliminate the impure. A group called the Obstructors helps the "impure" escape from Zone 7 and directs them to freedom and safety. Gramps has a radio on which they listen to "the evil empires of the world speak words of comfort" (p. 167), serving the functions of Radio Free Europe and the BBC during WWII.

We know that Zone 7 is "occupied territory" (p. 87), but its exact location is subtly revealed. Lines from the Anthem of the Motherland are presented as propaganda and repeated several times in the novel:

> *And once those feet did tread upon silver sand*
> *And footprints deep marked out new moons of Motherland*
> *Which all salute with upraised hand.* (p. 148)

It is not until the workers on the moon film set sing another version as rebellion after Standish reveals the hoax that this reader recognized Zone 7 as England:

> *And did those feet in ancient time . . .*
> *Walk upon England's mountains green.* (p. 275)

Although American readers may not recognize these lines from a poem by William Blake that was set to music by Sir Herbert Perry in 1916, English readers may realize the location of Zone 7 much earlier in the novel.

Vocabulary and Figurative Language

Fisher, Frey, and Lapp (2012) contend that when the language of a text varies from the reader's normal language usage, that text is more difficult. Some vocabulary in *Maggot Moon* is demanding for American readers because many words and word usages are common in England but not in the United States: for example, Standish observes that the "grass was Hoovered" (p. 6) and mentions a "lorry" (p. 9). In addition, the text contains words Standish apparently makes up or that reflect his dyslexia: He describes Hector's hair as "flopperty thick" (p. 64) and calls bigwigs "pigwigs" (p. 269). Perhaps one of the most challenging vocabulary demands is to figure out exactly what/ who the Greenflies are, especially since the illustrations feature what may be a greenfly.

Gardner expertly employs similes and metaphors as description, adding to the complexity of this text. Figurative language variously requires readers to apply their knowledge of the world or to create analogies and connections beyond the actual words. Early in the novel, Standish is called to the headmaster's office, where he first encounters the "leather-coat man" (p. 48). Although the headmaster "looked like a deflated zeppelin—all the hot air gone" (p. 51), the leather-coat man, who is about to interrogate Standish, wears his hat "knife sharp with a brim that could slice a lie in half" (p. 48).

The meaning of the standard phrases Standish misspeaks provides another vocabulary challenge. Resulting from his unique voice or his dyslexia, Standish alternately says, I'll "tell you this for a bucketful of tar" (p. 22), or "for a pocketful of dirt" (p. 37), or "for a bagful of humbugs" (p. 158). Confusing words, Standish imagines that landing on Juniper with Hector would be "humongous in the anus of history" (p. 61), and he believes Hector's father is "a bloody walking Cyclops" (p. 129) for knowing the exact distance between the earth and the moon.

Maggot Moon won the 2013 Carnegie Medal in the United Kingdom and a 2014 Michael L. Printz Honor Award, an award given annually to recognize the best young adult book. Although the quantitative demands of the text are appropriate for students in second or third grade, the qualitative demands and reader and task considerations deem this book more appropriate for older readers. Professional reviewers fittingly recommend this book for readers in grades 7 through 12.

Code Name Verity

Code Name Verity has a Lexile Measure of 1020 (Lexile, Metametrics, Inc.) based on sentence length and relative word frequency. This means it would be appropriate to expect proficient sixth through eighth grade students to successfully read and comprehend it. The qualitative factors somewhat support the quantitative evaluation of *Code Name Verity* and emphasize the importance of considering complexity through both technological and human measures. Thus, the complexity of *Code Name Verity* includes but surpasses sentence length and word frequency to lie in its unreliable and dual narration, unreliable character development, use of foreshadowing, specific vocabulary, and extensive cultural references.

Narration

The first two-thirds of the novel consist of a confession Queenie writes while imprisoned by the Gestapo. She writes repeatedly that she is a coward and that she is telling the truth. She begins by saying, "I wanted to be heroic and I pretended I was. I have always been good at pretending" (p. 1) and "I know I am a coward. And I'm going to give you anything you [Hauptsturmfüher Amadeus von Linden] ask, everything I can remember. Absolutely *Every Last Detail*" (p. 1).

She continues in this vein, berating herself for giving away important information: "I don't want to go down in history as the one who gave out the details" (p. 38), that this is the "most damning piece of information I've given you" (p. 41). She even confesses when she makes things up; when she explains the controls on an Anson she writes, "I'm making this up. You get the idea" (p. 94). She later writes, "I have told the truth. Isn't that ironic? They sent me because I am so good at telling lies. But I have told the truth" (pp. 200–201). At the end of her confession and probably her life, she hauntingly writes over and over: "I have told the truth" (pp. 201–2), and the reader has no reason to doubt her.

Queenie's rambling confession breaks Freytag's dramatic structure, increasing the complexity of the novel. She moves, often without signals, from codes and classified information to reminiscences of Maddie's story and of the horrors of her treatment in Château de Bordeaux. For example, under the heading "Aircraft Types," Queenie writes of the first time Maddie encountered a Puss Moth airplane piloted by a woman but digresses to a weekend she spent with Maddie. She drifts from one seemingly irrelevant detail to another:

> Maddie had a friend called Beryl who had left school, and in the summer of 1938 Beryl was working in the cotton mill at Ladderal, and they liked to take Sunday picnics on Maddie's motorbike because it was the only time they saw each other anymore. Beryl rode with her arms tight around Maddie's waist, like I did that time. No goggles for Beryl, or for me, though Maddie had her own. On this particular June Sunday they rode up through the lanes between the drystone walls that Beryl's laboring ancestors had built, and over the top of Highdown Rise, with mud up their bare shins. Beryl's best skirt was ruined that day, and her dad made her pay for a new one out of her next week's wages. (pp. 8–9)

Readers must sift through these digressions to get at the heart of the narrative.

Queenie focuses her confession on her friendship with Maddie. She writes it as Maddie's story, referring to herself in third person. When Fräulein Engel complains that Queenie is writing "irrelevant nonsense" (p. 57), von Linden recognizes her in the narrative and says "she flatters herself with competence and bravery that you have never witnessed. She is the young woman called Queenie, the wireless operator . . . our English agent" (pp. 57–58). Yet the point of view is inconsistent. She randomly switches back and forth between first and third person as she writes of her work as Eva Seiler.

The reader must sort out not only these changing points of view but also Queenie's various identities. She is Queenie, a WAAF wireless operator; Eva Seiler, Berlin's interpretive liaison and interrogator for British intelligence; Katharina Habicht, working with the French Resistance under the code name Verity; and ultimately Julie Lindsay MacKenzie Wallace Beaufort-Stuart of Craig Castle, Castle Craig, Scotland. A shifting point of view adds complexity to a text (Fisher, Frey, and Lapp, 2012), and this is especially so when a single narrator has multiple identities.

The point of view switches for the final third of the novel when Maddie takes over the narration under her alias, Kitty Hawk. Maddie's narrative is straightforward and chronological. At the beginning of her narrative, a double agent shows Maddie a picture of her crashed and burned plane the Gestapo will show Queenie. Maddie writes:

> If they have got Julie and they show her that picture, it will be a gift. She will make up an operator and a destination for every single one of those phony radios, and the frequencies and code sets to go with it. She will lead them blind. (pp. 232–33)

Her belief is confirmed when the confession Queenie wrote is smuggled out of the Château de Bordeaux. Maddie immediately recognizes that Queenie "could have told them *so much*, she knew So MUCH, and all she gave them was fake code" (p. 294). "She never told them ANYTHING" (p. 295). In a masterful plot twist, readers now know that Queenie embedded directions for blowing up the Gestapo headquarters in her fake confession, allowing the Resistance to complete the mission for which she was sent to France. Ultimately, the reader comes to understand that who s/he believed to be a traitorous reliable narrator is actually a courageous unreliable narrator.

Character Development

With the switch from Queenie's unreliable narration to Maddie's reliable one, readers see that not only is Queenie not who she seems to be, but also we have been misled about other characters as well. One such character is Georgia Penn, an American, pro-Fascist radio announcer based in Paris who has a show for Third Reich Radio called *No Place Like Home* broadcasting "rubbish . . . to make the American soldiers homesick" (p. 129).

Queenie calls her a "treacherous woman" (p. 129). Penn is granted an interview with Queenie to show "how unfeeling it is [for England] to use innocent girls as spies" (p. 242). Penn is obviously more than she seems in Queenie's account of the interview (pp. 129–36), yet it is not until Maddie's account that we learn that although Penn works for the Nazi Minister of Propaganda, she uses her position to go into prisons and prison camps to find people. She arranged the interview to find Verity. During the interview, Queenie adjusted her scarf (p. 130), crossed her legs, examined her wrist (p. 131), and tells Penn that "no one [is] suffering from arthritis *at all*" (p. 134).

Readers do not know until Maddie's account that by adjusting her scarf, crossing her legs, and examining her wrist, Queenie actually showed Penn physical signs of her torture, and her reference to arthritis conveyed that there was no broadcasting setup in the building. Although some novels can be "taken at face value," nothing is as it seems in complex texts, which are "more like onions, with layer upon layer of meaning" (Fisher, Frey, and Lapp, 2012, p. 49), which perfectly describes *Code Name Verity*.

Fräulein Engle is another character who is one person in Queenie's narrative and another in Maddie's. Queenie writes repeatedly of the abuse she suffers at the hands of "the evil Engle" (p. 63), who engages in small acts of torture (pp. 11, 19, 39, 129, 150) and uses her training as a chemist to engage in more horrific acts. Queenie refers to her as a "fount of information" (p. 113): information about the likelihood that she will be sent to Ravensbrück or Natzweiler-Struthof to be used as a live specimen for medical experiments. Engle also tells her she is classified as "*Nacht und Nebel*" (p. 103), meaning that she will simply disappear without a trace into the "night and fog."

Yet during Maddie's narration, we learn that Engle is actually Queenie's "angel" (p. 262) and later an "avenging angel" (p. 307), passing on Queenie's coded confession, an archive number for blueprints of the building (p. 306), and a service door key (p. 309) so the Resistance can complete the mission of blowing up the Château de Bordeaux.

One particular inconsistency relates to cigarettes. Queenie writes that "a lit cigarette is such a convenient accessory if your job happens to be Extracting Information from Enemy Intelligence Agents" (pp. 63–64), but Engle never offered her one out of kindness. Yet Engle tells Maddie, "I damn well gave her half my salary in cigarettes, greedy little Scottish savage! She nearly bankrupted me" (p. 308). Again, Queenie's veiled her confession to protect herself and Engle, and they "created it between them" (p. 298)—contradiction upon contradiction and complexity upon complexity.

Foreshadowing

Much of the complexity rests in the fact that the "truth" is not visible until Maddie's reveal, requiring readers to recognize patterns retroactively "casting backward . . . connecting what we're currently reading to what we read before" (Barnhouse and Vinton, 2012, p. 113). Details that seem innocuous become critical long after they have been read. Hindsight makes foreshadowing that was previously invisible, suddenly visible. Foreshadowing makes the text harder because of time shifts (Fisher, Frey, and Lapp, 2012), but it is particularly powerful in relation to the climax of *Code Name Verity*.

Queenie and Maddie discuss the moral dilemmas they both face as a result of their war work. Queenie envies Maddie "the simplicity of her work, the spiritual cleanness of it. . . . There was no guilt, no moral dilemma, no argument or anguish" (p. 140) in contrast to her work interrogating prisoners. Yet

Maddie sees it differently: "I'm not blameless. . . . Every bomber I deliver goes operational and kills people" (p. 165). We later understand that Maddie faces the ultimate moral dilemma.

In Queenie's narrative, she explores the concept of mercy killings as she relates a family story to Maddie. Maddie had just shared her fear of letting people down, and Queenie told of a great-uncle who suffered from throat cancer and finally "asked his wife to kill him, and she did" (p. 77). She argued that her great-aunt did him a favor by killing him and that "you'd let them down if you *didn't*" (p. 77).

When Maddie reads the confession, she does not remember Queenie ever telling her this story and believes Queenie "put in the great-aunt story because she thought we might have to blow the place up with her inside" (p. 299). Contemplating her fate at Ravensbrück or Natzweiler-Struthof, Queenie muses, "If I am very lucky—I mean if I am clever about it—I will get myself shot" (p. 113). Concurrently, Maddie learns to shoot using a "Double Tap system" (p. 217), and when they believe Julie may have been guillotined, Maddie "WON'T believe she's dead until I hear the shots MYSELF and see her fall" (p. 268). This complex foreshadowing prepares unsuspecting readers for the story's climax.

Vocabulary

The vocabulary in *Code Name Verity* places specific demands on the reader since Wein uses a sophisticated general vocabulary (*parsimoniously* [p. 49], *effluvium* [p. 87], *eiderdown* [p. 105], and *prosaically* [p. 145]), words specifically used in the United Kingdom (*brolly* [p. 49] and *scarpered* [p. 316]), and military acronyms and terms (*RAF*, *WAAF*, and *AT*). References to geographical locations in England, Scotland, and France place unique demands on the reader who may not be familiar with these mountains, rivers, and cities, some of which are real and others of which are fictional. Integrated passages in French, German, and Gaelic demand readers infer meaning through context.

Cultural References

Cultural references contribute to the novel's complexity. One of the primary references is to *Peter Pan*, J. M. Barrie's 1911 novel. Maddie and Queenie repeatedly quote the line "Second to the right and then straight on till morning" (pp. 68, 91, 124, 174) when giving directions. As Queenie writes her confession, she names a young pilot Michael "after the youngest of the Darling children in *Peter Pan*" (p. 154), and the flight that takes Queenie into France is "Operation Dogstar" (p. 174).

When the BBC announces to the Resistance that Verity is on her way, they broadcast *"Tous les enfants, sauf un, grandissent"*—the first line of Peter Pan, "All children, except one, grow up" (p. 175). At Craig Castle, Lady Beaufort-Stuart always "leaves a window open in her children's bedrooms when they're away" (p. 227). Perhaps the most important cultural reference is to Lord Horatio Nelson's dying words at the Battle of Trafalger, "Kiss me, Hardy!"(p. 68). Queenie uses this quote when she needs to summon courage (pp. 100, 197), and shouts it as her final coded message and act of defiance.

Code Name Verity was named an honor book for the 2012 Boston Globe-Horn Book Award and the 2013 Michael L. Printz Award, and it was short-listed for the United Kingdom's 2013 Carnegie Medal, the 2012 Scottish Children's Book Award, and Australia's 2013 Silver Inky. Professional reviewers recommend this book for readers in grades 9 through 12. Quantitative dimensions, qualitative dimensions, and reader and task considerations validate this recommendation.

BRINGING TOGETHER THE BOOK AND THE READER

Selecting complex texts for use in the content classroom requires more than finding a "hard" book. Teachers must read the text carefully to assess its qualitative and quantitative dimensions and take the reader and task into consideration. Each of these areas, equally important to the students' comprehension of the text, requires deliberate teacher attention. Knowing the reader and the book allows teachers to select texts that will challenge students intellectually, increase their knowledge, expose them to new vocabulary, and prompt higher-level thinking. At the same time, knowing the reader and knowing the book enables teachers to provide students with the support they need to independently demonstrate the type of cognitive expertise complex text requires. Students need and deserve the opportunity to interact with complex text.

REFERENCES

Adams, M. J. (2009). The challenge of advanced texts. In E. H. Hiebert (ed.), *Reading more, reading better* (pp. 163–89). New York, NY: The Guilford Press.

Atwell, N. (2007). *The reading zone: How to help kids become skilled, passionate, habitual, critical readers*. New York, NY: Scholastic.

Barnhouse, D., and Vinton, V. (2012). *What readers really do: Teaching the process of meaning making*. Portsmouth, NH: Heinemann.

Cazden, C. B. (2001). *Classroom discourse: The language of teaching and learning* (2nd ed.). Portsmouth, NH: Heinemann.

Fisher, D., Frey, N., and Lapp, D. (2012). *Text complexity: Raising rigor in reading.* Newark, DE: International Reading Association.

Fry, E. (2002). Readability versus leveling. *The Reading Teacher, 56*(3), 286–91.

Galda, L., and Graves, M. F. (2006). *Reading and responding in the middle grades: Approaches for all classrooms.* Boston, MA: Pearson.

Gallagher, K. (2009). *Readicide: How schools are killing reading and what you can do about it.* Portland, ME: Stenhouse.

Gardner, S. (2013). *Maggot Moon.* Illus. by Julian Crouch. Somerville, MA: Candlewick.

Guthrie, J. T., and Davis, M. H. (2003). Motivating struggling readers in a middle school through an engagement model of classroom practice. *Reading and Writing Quarterly, 19*, 59–85.

Guthrie, J. T., and Humenick, N. M. (2004). Motivating students to read: Evidence for classroom practices that increase reading motivation and achievement. In P. McCardle and V. Chhabra (eds.), *The voice of evidence in reading research* (pp. 329–54). Baltimore, MD: Paul H. Brookes.

Hancock, M. R. (2008). *A celebration of literature and response: Children, books, and teachers in K–8 classrooms* (3rd ed.). Upper Saddle River, NJ: Pearson.

Kelley, M. J., Wilson, N. S., and Koss, M. D. (2012). Using young adult literature to motivate and engage the disengaged. In J. A. Hayn and J. S. Kaplan (eds.), *Teaching young adult literature today* (pp. 79–97). Lanham, MD: Rowman & Littlefield.

Lesesne, T. S. (2003). *Making the match: The right book for the right reader at the right time, grades 4–12.* Portland, ME: Stenhouse.

Miller, D., and Kelley, S. (2014). *Reading in the wild: The book whisperer's keys to cultivating lifelong reading habits.* San Francisco, CA: Jossey-Bass.

Moley, P. F., Bandré, P. E., and George, J. E. (2011). Moving beyond readability: Considering choice, motivation, and reader engagement. *Theory Into Practice, 50*, 247–53. doi:10.1080/00405841.2011.58406.

Pitcher, S. M., Albright, L. K., DeLaney, C. J., Walker, N. T., Seunarinesingh, K., Mogge, S., et al. (2007). Assessing adolescents' motivation to read. *Journal of Adolescent and Adult Literacy, 50*(5), 378–96. doi:10.1598/JAAL.50.5.5.

Schussler, D. L. (2009). Beyond content: How teachers manage classrooms to facilitate intellectual engagement for disengaged students. *Theory Into Practice, 48*, 114–21.

Wein, E. (2012). *Code Name Verity.* New York, NY: Hyperion.

Chapter Four

Exploring Point of View and Narration in Young Adult Literature

Connecting Teen Readers with Multiple Narrator Books

Terrell A. Young, Nancy L. Hadaway, and Barbara A. Ward

Authors use a mode of narration—point of view—to provide readers with insight into their stories. Point of view uses characters' actions and behaviors as well as their thoughts and dialogue, to let readers see and hear what is taking place in the story. According to Lukens (2007), "Whose view of the story the writer tells determines the point of view. Who sees the events determines how the story will develop" (p. 169).

Authors manipulate point of view to influence how readers interpret the text. Aronson (2001) notes that most YA books have been written in the first- or third-person point of view; however, there are radical changes afoot with authors today telling stories from multiple, often competing, points of view.

Koss and Teale (2009) examined a sample of recent books drawn from award winners including the Printz Award and Honor books, YA favorite lists such as Young Adults' Choices, and best-seller lists, and they note that "almost one in every four books was written using either a combination of first and third person or multiple voices/multiple narrators alternating to tell the story and thus provide multiple points of view" (p. 568). Serafini and Blasingame (2012) suggest that when novels are told from multiple perspectives, "Different versions of the world blur together as readers have to consider not only what is told, but also from whose perspective the events are rendered" (p. 147).

Studying the choices authors make as they write books gives readers insights into the actions, conversations, and thoughts of each book's characters. In this chapter the authors explore both prose and verse novels that include multiple and combined narration in contemporary YA fiction for grades 6 through 12 published in the United States and abroad, and highlight

51

how these new formats offer an excellent opportunity to focus on CCSS Anchor Standard 6, assessing how point of view or purpose shapes the content and style of a text.

TYPES OF POINT OF VIEW

Writers determine the type of point of view when they choose who will narrate the story and how much the narrator knows (Lukens, 2007). Typically authors employ four types of point of view—first person, omniscient, limited omniscient, and objective or dramatic.

In the first-person point of view, the story is told in the first-person "I" by either the protagonist or a "minor character who observes the action and tells what the protagonist is doing" (Lukens, 2007, p. 170). For instance, Shannon Hale chose to narrate her book *Dangerous* (2014) through the voice, thoughts, and observations of the protagonist, Maisie Danger Brown. The first lines of the book indicate the point of view: "Every superhero has an origin story. Mine began with a box of cereal" (p. 5). In this science fiction story, the protagonist receives her first superpower as a "token" enters her body.

> White-hot cold piercing my hand, stealing my breath. I heard someone scream and someone else say, "owie, owie, owie . . . ," but I couldn't look away from the token thing submerging as if my palm were water. I clawed at it with Ms. Pincher's plastic fingers.
>
>   The ripping pain stabbed into my wrist and crawled up my arm, tearing through my shoulder and thudding into my chest, where it flared to a point of agony that killed every thought from my head. (Hale, 2014, p. 63)

The first-person narration helps readers identify with the character, making the story seem more immediate and real (Lukens, 2007). These narrators are not always traditional human characters, nor are they always reliable. For instance, in Deborah Ellis's *The Cat on the Wall* (2014), the book is narrated by a cat, and in Markus Zusak's *The Book Thief* (2006), Death is the narrator.

With omniscient point of view, the writer is "omniscient about any and every detail of action, thought and feeling—conscious or unconscious—in the past, present, or future" (Lukens, 2007, p. 170). This type of narration is ideal for Sarah Mlynowski's *Don't Even Think about It* (2014), in which nearly an entire tenth grade homeroom class could hear the thoughts of others nearby after receiving flu shots. Not only does the book have an "all-knowing narrator," but the class members also contribute to the narration.

Sometimes the narration is a collective "we" that represents the thoughts of all of those who have the ability to hear others' thoughts. For example, "We can't help wondering if she wanted to lose him all along" (p. 39). At other times the thoughts of individual students are shared in italics.

> Olivia looked around the room. Everyone was talking, but no one was moving his or her lips.
> *What's wrong with her?*
> *She looks like she's going to barf.*
> *Oh. My. God.* They were not saying these things, Olivia realized. They were thinking them. She was hearing what people were thinking, and they were all thinking about her. The shock was so strong, she could barely breathe. (pp. 31–32)

The omniscient point of view allows the reader to know everything, which is essential to the plot of *Don't Even Think about It.*

Another point of view that authors employ is the limited omniscient point of view. Here the writer tells the story through the eyes of one character (or a few characters). "The writer shows not only what the character sees and hears, but also what the character feels and believes. The writer is inside as well as alongside the character" (Lukens, 2007, p. 176).

In Teresa Flavin's *The Shadow Lantern* (2014), readers have access not only to actions and conversations, but also to Sunni's thoughts and explanations of why she says and does some things. For example, she tells Blaise about her plans:

> "I'm going to Mandy's birthday party," she said.
> "Oh, yeah?"
> "Yeah. It's a sleepover."
> "Bunch of girls, then."
> "So?"
> "So . . . nothing." Blaise finally looked up at her. "I guess you're not grounded any more if you can go to a party." (Flavin, 2014, p. 2)

The narrator then explains why Sunni had lied and said that she was grounded:

> Sunni hadn't been able to tell Blaise that her parents blamed him for getting them in trouble during their visit to London, so she had said she was grounded. After a while he stopped asking her when she'd be free to hang out again. That's when she started to lie to Rhona and her dad. (Flavin, 2014, p. 3)

"In the objective or dramatic point of view, the writer does not enter the minds of any of the characters. The action speaks for itself as it unfolds and the reader hears speeches and sees action" (Lukens, 2007, p. 178). An example of objective point of view is found in Lauren Myracle's *yolo* (2014), where the story is told through instant messaging. Readers will find that the characters from *ttyl* (2004) are now in college.

> mad maddie: but just cuz we're growing up doesn't mean we have to grow apart.
>
> Snow Angel: Maddie, that's so corny! you're so adorable!!!
>
> mad maddie: and with that in mind, I have a plan for keeping us together.
>
> Snow Angel: does it include finishing my business hw for me? cuz shocking as it is, I would actually NOT like to weigh in on how modern control theory is used in evaluating economic conditions;
>
> Snow Angel: MY BUSINESS CLASS IS SOOOOOO BORING!
>
> mad maddie: I feel for you. back to what *I* was saying. I just think we shld—
> (Myracle, 2014, p. 3)

Myracle provides readers with the digital conversations, but the readers must draw conclusions about the girls' unwritten thoughts and feelings.

RECENT TRENDS IN POINT OF VIEW AND NARRATION

As noted, recent trends in young adult literature have included combined narration, a technique that gives readers insight into several characters (Koss, 2009; Koss and Teale, 2009). "These books challenge the traditional linear, chronological, and single-voiced nature of narrative fiction, which (a) is typically told from the first-person point of view of the main character, or (b) focuses on a main character but is written in third person" (Koss, 2009, p. 74).

Koss (2009) interviewed three different populations (teens, professionals in the field of YA literature, and young adult publishing) to determine the reasons for the increase in the publication of multiple-perspective young adult novels. Three themes emerged: textual changes, teen changes, and technological changes. In terms of textual changes, the respondents felt that this new trend in YA literature reflected "the changing nature of society, which is becoming more accepting of diverse populations and multiple perspectives on single events" (p. 77). Teen changes were also reflective of the changing society as adolescents develop and grow up faster, hence "multiple narrative perspectives may be written as a form of bibliotherapy, or to provide teens with a picture of other teens who may be going through similar life events" (p. 77).

Finally, technology has brought so many changes to contemporary society. These new formats mirror the nonlinear format of webpages and other nonprint media on which young people increasingly rely. Also, the multiple perspectives provided in many books resemble the barrage of information that readers today must sort through on a daily basis to reach decisions and to be fully informed.

Gillis (2002) describes multiple-narrator novels with the following analogy: "The quick jumps from perspective to perspective are like a cinematic montage, creating atmosphere, revealing relationships, and building tension" (p. 53). Indeed, the books examined for this chapter reflect not only alternating narrators but also diverse geographic settings and time periods as well as interdisciplinary perspectives such as AIDS, adoption, single parenting, and medical practices in the seventeenth century.

In her analysis of recent YA literature, Koss (2009, p. 76) identified several categories of multiple-narrative-perspective novels including the following:

• one event, multiple perspectives
• one story, multiple perspectives
• multiple stories, multiple perspectives intertwined
• then and now, and
• parallel stories.

Reflecting the one-event, multiple-perspectives format, deeper understanding of major historical events such as the sinking of the Titanic, the 1889 Johnstown Flood, and the construction of the Panama Canal arises from the many-faceted viewpoints in *The Watch That Ends the Night: Voices from the Titanic* (Wolf, 2011), *Three Rivers Rising: A Novel of the Johnstown Flood* (Richards, 2010), and *Silver People: Voices from the Panama Canal* (Engle, 2014). All of these novels attest to the different attitudes toward social classes and economic status in the past.

Seemingly, no perspective of those aboard the Titanic is left unexplored in *The Watch That Ends the Night,* even that of a rat scurrying about the ship in search of food and shelter as the great ship sinks into the Atlantic waters. Similarly, the forest and animals in *Silver People: Voices from the Panama Canal* share their concerns about the encroachment of the workers, machines, and explosives.

One story is revealed through multiple perspectives in *Newes from the Dead* (Hooper, 2008), set in seventeenth-century England. Chapters alternate between an Oxford medical student and an innocent young woman, presumed dead after hanging, who awakens on the dissection table. Additionally, the chapters move between the present as the doctors prepare for the dissection unaware that their "cadaver" is actually alive, and the past as the young woman's mind races through flashbacks reconstructing the situation that led to her being sentenced to hanging.

Lindsey Lane's *Evidence of Things Not Seen* (2014) is another example of one story told through multiple perspectives. In this book for middle school or junior high students, a boy disappears and multiple characters express their ideas about what happened. The book's open ending makes this book ideal for classroom discussions about what really happened. Students can share and "defend their opinions in conversations and in writing and exploring new ideas through response logs and discussion boards" (Searfini and Blasingame, 2014, p. 147). Such activity not only makes learning more interesting, but also helps them progress in the CCSS curriculum as they learn to use text to support their ideas.

Multiple stories and multiple perspectives are interwoven in Steven Herrick's verse novel *Cold Skin* (2009). Nine characters describe life in a small post–World War II coal mining town in Australia. The main focus is on the Holding family as the two brothers struggle to define themselves while their father wrestles with anger and guilt about his lack of combat service in the war. Then a young schoolgirl is murdered, and the secrets and misbehaviors of several of the townsfolk surface.

Two parallel stories are told by alternating narrators in the prose novel *The Girl Who Saw Lions* (Doherty, 2008). Chapters juxtapose Abela, a young Tanzanian orphan, and Rose, a young girl in London whose single mother wants to adopt a child. Readers follow along as Abela struggles with grief as her father, mother, and young sister die of AIDS and her uncle sends her to England as a pawn in his illegal plans. All the while, young Rose grapples with the idea of sharing her life and her mother with another sibling. Eventually, the two stories are woven together when the two girls meet.

In *Etched in Clay* (Cheng, 2013), the story of Dave the Potter is told in multiple voices, and stretches over seven decades, beginning in 1801 with Dr. Abner Landrum, who sends his nephew off to buy a slave to help in his pottery work, and ending in 1870 as David Drake (once known only as Dave the Potter) ruminates on his past. As Dave learns to read, staring "at the pages, / struggling to make sense / of the letters, / until one day / they jump off the page!" (p. 35), reading and writing offer him an avenue to express his feelings. Cruelly, even that small joy is taken from him through restrictive literacy laws, and Dave "cannot stop the words from flowing. . . . But I don't write them down, / and the words float away / like twigs in a stream, / stuck on a rock / for a moment / and then gone" (p. 95).

CONNECTING COMMON CORE STATE STANDARDS AND YA LITERATURE

While multiple-perspective novels may mirror contemporary society, some students may find such novels difficult to read. "The multiple genres or narratives may seem a jumble of disconnected voices, devoid of the familiar 'coherence' of identifiable protagonists, antagonists, settings, linear chronology, and clear beginnings, middles, and ends" (Gillis, 2002, p. 55). Thus, as Gillis argues, the reader must become more active, take on some of the narrative task, and assume more authority over the text.

"They are thrust into the position of reporters, detectives, or juries hearing testimonies. They must review evidence and draw patterns from what they see and hear, actively constructing meaning" (p. 56). Explicitly connecting the Common Core State Standards and multiple-perspective novels can help. In this section, the authors discuss several combined-narration novels and how they can address each standard within Craft and Structure: Anchor 6, English Language Arts Standards: Reading Literature: Assess how point of view or purpose shapes the content and style of a text. As students move across the grade levels, they will experience two aspects of point of view—narration and character perspective (Linder, 2012). The earlier grades focus on narration and the later grades build on narration to emphasize character perspective.

Grade 6: Explain how an author develops the point of view of the narrator or speaker in a text. Whether authors choose a single narrator or multiple points of view to tell the story, they make choices in order to develop the point of view of the narrator(s). For instance, as previously discussed, authors choose the distance of the narrator from the story (e.g., first-, second-, or third-person narration), and they also decide how much to reveal about the thoughts and feelings of the characters.

In *Son of a Gun* (deGraaf, 2012), the author uses first-person narration for the two protagonists, Lucky and Nopi, who tell their stories about the violence of war in Liberia. In this way, the readers are able to develop empathy and to feel more deeply how war affects innocent children. For instance, when Nopi, the young girl, attempts to protect her brother, a soldier strikes her across her ear with the butt of his rifle and she falls and hits her head and other ear on a rock. At first, she is stunned. Then, she is forced into a difficult realization.

I had to remember, and with that memory came understanding. I put a hand up to touch my ear and felt warm blood. I looked down as it caked my shoulder. It felt like someone had stuck a knife through my head, in one ear and out the other. I opened my mouth and felt my throat open and close, but I heard nothing! Not my voice, not the cries of the boys beside me, not the birds in the trees, nothing! (p. 24)

The reader feels Nopi's pain but also suffers with her brother, Lucky, as he bears the weight of guilt. He grieves, "My sister is deaf because of me. This thought waited for me every day like a lion waiting for its prey" (p. 27).

In contrast, Harnett (2011) uses third-person omniscient narration in *The Midnight Zoo* to create a complex story that addresses different perspectives on war. In this novel, readers are provided access to the thoughts and feelings of two young Romany boys as well as a host of zoo animals, all trapped by war. Their interactions and dialogue offer a powerful story about war and freedom from different, yet similar, perspectives.

Grade 7: Analyze how an author develops and contrasts the points of view of different characters or narrators in a text. DeGraaf (2012) develops and contrasts the points of view of two narrators, a brother and sister, in *Son of a Gun.* Age is a factor in point of view as the older sister, Nopi, feels responsible for protecting her young brother and she also vaguely remembers a time before war, or at least the stories of happier times from her grandmother. However, Lucky has never known a life without violence and conflict in Liberia. And he, too, feels responsibility when his youth and inexperience result in an injury to his sister.

Gender also influences how the war shapes the perspectives of each of the narrators. Lucky, the young boy, is forced into service as a child soldier. As he describes, "Yeah, I was forced to kill others. No way I'll ever be welcome back in any of the villages we attacked. I don't think my parents even want to know what I've done, and I'm not going to tell them. Why would I? I want to be loved" (p. 88).

Nopi must serve in another way. She is captured by a rebel soldier and not only sent into battle but also forced to be one of his wives. She explains, "I don't love him. I would have run away the very first night, but his second wife, a girl younger than me . . . told me he would cut off my arms if they caught me" (p. 66). Eventually, Nopi does escape.

The Midnight Zoo (Hartnett, 2011) contrasts the point of view of different characters—two young boys who have lost their family and must flee their Romany encampment with that of animals in a zoo abandoned by their keeper due to the war and locked in their cages without food or water. Several interchanges, such as the following example, explore two important questions: Who is trapped? Who is free?

> "*Wah-wah-wah,*" said the chamois. "No life is without its troubles, kid, not even the life of a rat. Look on the bright side: you aren't in a cage. You're free, so stop complaining."
>
> Andrej said, "No, I'm not in a cage, but—I don't feel free. If you're free, you should be safe. And I don't feel safe. I always feel . . . hunted."
>
> "Boo-hoo," said the chamois rancorously. "Talk to me about being hunted when you find your foot in a snare, little buck."
>
> The llama's tufted ears turned: "How peculiar! You can go anywhere your feet take you, and yet you're not free. There are no bars around you, yet you're in a funny kind of cage. *That* isn't fair."
>
> "Cages come and get you," murmured the kangaroo. (pp. 163–64)

Grade 8: Analyze how differences in the points of view of the characters and the audience or reader (e.g., created through the use of dramatic irony) create such effects as suspense or humor. In *The Midnight Zoo*, Harnett (2011) creates humor with the differences in perspectives and power structure among the animals in the zoo. For example, the lioness has lost her cubs so she asks Andrej to bring his baby sister close to her cage so she can check on her.

> "Bring her to me," said the cat. "I'd rather see for myself."
> From across the lawn came a wry bleating laugh. "I wouldn't do that if I were you, kid! Not unless you want to see a lioness eat her dinner!"
> The lioness showed a glimpse of tooth. "Quiet, goat."
> The chamois bounced forward. "I am not a goat."
> "Shush, both of you!" whimpered the llama. . . .
> "She *must* not call me a goat! It's disrespectful!"
> "Disrespectful to goats," said the lioness, and the monkey sniggered. (pp. 48–49)

Harnett also creates a sense of the irony of our actions when the wolf explains the reason for the bombing of their village: "[The villagers] could not do nothing. This land was their home, their territory. They *had* to fight for it. Never mind that *their* kind have seized so much *wolf* territory, cut down our trees, set traps in our ground, caved in our dens, pursued us to—" (p. 58). Further, there is both irony and humor in one interchange between the wolf and the younger Romany boy:

> The wolf spoke up. "I've told you the reason for everything that happens. Somebody decides they will have their way."
> "And it has to happen, even if their way is wrong?" . . . "I don't think that's right, wolf. What if you're smarter than they are? Sometimes you can win by being smarter than everyone else."
> "I am smarter than you," replied the wolf, "yet I am locked in this cage, and you're walking around free."
> Tomas grinned. "That must mean I'm mightier than you."
> "Well," said the wolf, "we could decide that, if you let me out." (p. 146)

Grades 9–10: Analyze a particular point of view or cultural experience reflected in a work of literature from outside the United States, drawing on a wide reading of world literature. Son of a Gun (deGraaf, 2012) was published originally in the Netherlands and later in the United States. The prose novel takes place in Liberia and deals with war and its impact on children who are caught up in the violence and exploitation of war as well as enduring the effects of war such as refugee camps and the separation of families. In the beginning of the story, Nopi makes a poignant plea for global understanding as she notes,

> "I've heard about your side of the world, you know. . . . I wonder if there's a place for my story in your world. People say a lot of things about Africa. Maybe you could shut out those voices now, and just listen with your heart." "Hey, we're just like you, you know. Well, okay, maybe a little different color, and a whole lot warmer, but you want to bet we're not afraid of the same things." (pp. 11–12)

Hartnett's *The Midnight Zoo,* published first in Australia and then in the United States, also depicts the effects of war. While the specific war is not explicitly stated, readers are led to believe that this story takes place during World War II with the mention of soldiers who use German phrases. This story also highlights a part of World War II that has not been fully explored, namely the discrimination and persecution of the Romany (gypsy) people.

This anti-Romany sentiment is painfully evident during one incident when an old woman tries to take baby Wilma from the two brothers under the guise of helping them (p. 158). "Keep her then!" the ghastly stranger had shouted. "The soldiers will take care of her! They're looking for people like you. Dirty little leeches. Filthy nasty robbers. Vermin, you are! Heathen vermin! The sooner they get rid of the likes of you, the better off we'll be."

Grades 11–12: Analyze a case in which grasping a point of view requires distinguishing what is directly stated in a text from what is really meant (e.g., satire, sarcasm, irony, or understatement). In *The Midnight Zoo,* the animals in the zoo are the innocent victims of human actions that led to war as the lioness points out:

> "I do not think my cubs will remember me," said the lioness, "when they are grown, as you are." Tomas, who had shrunk behind his brother, emerged and spoke up timorously. "I'm sad that the lion and your cubs were taken away because of the war."
> The lioness's eyes turned toward him. Her head was a magnificent thing, like the head of the sun. Her long willowy body was supple and strong as a river. "Because of your war," she said. (p. 118)

In Deborah Wiles's *Revolution* (2014), the second title in her Sixties trilogy, the story of the civil rights movement is told from the points of view of two characters, one white and one black, whose lives briefly touch during an explosive period of our nation's history. Sunny is a child of privilege who is annoyed once the public pools are closed for the summer to prevent them from being integrated, while Raymond is a talented baseball player who has quietly endured the prejudices of his life and now finds hope in daring to take a stand. "So I make up my mind. I need somebody to take notice" (p. 155).

Additional Young Adult Multiple-Narrator Books

Baskin, N. R. (2014). *Subway love*. Somerville, MA: Candlewick.

Bryant, J. (2008). *Ringside 1925: Views from the Scopes trial*. New York, NY: Knopf Books for Young Readers.

Christopher, L. (2014). *The killing woods*. New York, NY: Scholastic/Chickenhouse.

Clark, K. E. (2013). *Freakboy*. New York, NY: Farrar, Straus and Giroux.

Croggon, A. (2013). *Black spring*. Somerville, MA: Candlewick.

Ellis, D. (2014). *Moon at nine*. Toronto, ON: Pajama Press.

Engle, M. (2013). *The lightning dreamer*. Boston, MA: Houghton Mifflin Harcourt.

Flake, S. G. (2012). *Pinned*. New York, NY: Scholastic.

Frost, H. (2009). *Crossing stones*. New York, NY: Farrar, Straus, and Giroux.

Giles, G. (2014). *Girls like us*. Somerville, MA: Candlewick.

Henry, A. (2014). *The body in the woods*. New York, NY: Henry Holt and Company.

Hopkins. E. (2011). *Perfect*. New York, NY: Margaret K. McElderry Books.

Hopkins. E. (2011). *Triangle*. New York, NY: Margaret K. McElderry Books.

Hopkins, E. (2012). *Collateral*. New York, NY: Atria Publishing/Simon and Schuster.

Hopkins, E. (2012). *Tilt*. New York, NY: Margaret K. McElderry Books.

Hopkins, E. (2013). *Smoke*. New York, NY: Simon & Schuster/Margaret A. McElderry Books.

Klass, D., and Klass, P. (2014). *Second impact*. New York, NY: Farrar, Straus and Giroux.

Kortege, R. (2014). *The Brimstone journals*. Somerville, MA: Candlewick Press.

Laybourne, E. (2014). *Savage drift*. New York, NY: Feiwel & Friends.

Magoon, K. (2014). *How it went down*. New York, NY: Henry Holt.

Additional Young Adult Multiple-Narrator Books

Mathieu, J. (2014). *The truth about Alice*. New York, NY: Roaring Brook Press.

Moses, J. A. (2014). *Tales from my closet*. New York, NY: Scholastic.

Myracle, L. (2014). *The infinite moment of us*. New York, NY: AbramsAmulet.

Newman, L. (2012). *October mourning: A song for Matthew Shepard*. Somerville, MA: Candlewick.

Rowell, R. (2013). *Eleanor & Park*. New York, NY: Macmillan/St. Martin's Press.

Schmidt, G. D. (2012). *What came from the stars*. New York, NY: Clarion.

Schroeder, L. (2010). *Chasing Brooklyn*. New York, NY: Simon Pulse.

Schroeder, L. (2014). *The bridge from me to you*. New York, NY: Point.

Sloan, H. G. (2014. *Just call my name*. New York, NY: Little, Brown Books for Young Readers.

Smith, J. E. (2014). *The geography of you and me*. New York, NY: Little, Brown Books for Young Readers/Poppy.

Standiford, N. (2014). *Switched at birthday*. New York, NY: Scholastic.

Stiefvater, M. (2014). *Sinner*. New York, NY: Scholastic.

Taschjian, J. (2012). *For what it is worth*. New York, NY: Henry Holt.

Terrill, C. (2013). *All our yesterdays*. New York, NY: Disney/Hyperion.

Whitman, S. (2013). *The milk of birds*. New York, NY: Atheneum Books for Young Readers.

Figure 4.1.

Meanwhile, Sunny also wants to be noticed by her family and her mother, who abandoned her many years ago, and she finds herself attracted to the revolution that is building in her small town. "Believe me, there are only so many times that you can sing 'I've got the joy, joy, joy, joy down in my heart' before you have no more joy at all, anywhere. None. Zero. It's already as hot as blue blazes in the sixth-grade Sunday school room, and all I can feel is the hot-hot-hot-hot down to my toes. I cannot believe I'm sitting here. I didn't have any joy to begin with" (p. 155). Interestingly, Wiles has chosen not to identify the narrative shifts by shading the pages that contain Ray's thoughts.

GRAPHIC ORGANIZERS FOR TEACHING

Graphic organizers are often helpful for teaching new skills, strategies, or content. These organizers have three basic functions (McLaughlin, 2012): (1) to provide a visual model of the text or strategy, (2) to scaffold the students' text comprehension, and (3) to provide students with a place to document text evidence to support their positions. Supporting students through the use of graphic organizers seems especially appropriate for books with multiple perspectives because such books, as Koss (2009, p. 77) notes, "are also complex, pushing readers to follow several different strands, sometimes out of chronological/linear order; readers must also adjust to different voices and/ or narrators, sometimes through switching of tenses, and occasionally juggle conflicting information from unreliable narrators."

McLaughlin and Overturf (2013) suggest the following steps scaffolding students' use of graphic organizers.

1. First . . .explain how the organizer works.
2. Next . . . demonstrate how to use it.
3. Then . . . engage students in guided practice [working with partners].
4. After that, students practice on their own.
5. Finally . . . engage students in reflection about how to use the organizer, what they have learned, [and how the organizer helped them]. (p. 1)

Teachers can adjust these steps to meet the needs of their students. The authors have developed graphic organizers that can be adapted for teaching narration and point of view to adolescent students.

CONCLUSION

This chapter serves as a model to middle and high school teachers to illustrate how readers' comprehension is deepened when they consider how point of view shapes their reading experiences. New formats in young adult literature offer an excellent opportunity to focus on CCSS Anchor Standard 6. Students can assess how point of view or purpose shapes the content and style of a text. "We can help our students be successful at reading these novels by helping them become more conscious of the strategies required by their new reading role" (Gillis, 2002, p. 56).

Character and Plot Revelation	Text Evidence
Character Thoughts	
Narrator's Description	
Dialogue	
Character Actions	

Who tells the story?

What is the type of point of view? Why?

Figure 4.2.

Character Names		
Beliefs		
Values		
Attitudes		
Actions		
Perspective		

How is one character's point of view (or perspective) different from the other's?

Figure 4.3.

What the Author Wrote	What It Really Meant

Explain the irony.

How did it create humor or suspense?

Figure 4.4.

Analyzing Point of View and Culture	
What is the main point of view in the story?	Evidence?
What does this point of view tell us about the culture being depicted in the book?	Evidence?
How might the story be different if it had been set in the United States?	Evidence?
What points of view are missing from the story? How might their inclusion change the story?	Evidence?

Figure 4.5.

What the Author Wrote (include page numbers)	What It Really Meant

Explain how this is an example of satire, sarcasm, irony, or understatement.

Figure 4.6.

REFERENCES

Aronson, M. (2001). *Exploding the myths: The truth about teenagers and reading.* Lanham, MD: Scarecrow.

Gillis, C. (2002). Multiple voices, multiple genres: Fiction for young adults. *The English Journal, 92*(2), 52–59.

Koss, M. D. (2009). Young adult novels with multiple narrative perspectives. *The ALAN Review, 36*(3), 73–80.

Koss, M. D., and Teale, W. H. (2009). What's happening in YA literature? Trends in books for adolescents. *Journal of Adolescent and Adult Literacy, 52*(7), 563–72.

Linder, R. (2012). Common core and point of view. Retrieved from http://ontheweb .rozlinder.com/common-core-and-point-of-view.

Lukens, R. J. (2007). *A critical handbook of children's literature.* Boston, MA: Allyn & Bacon/Pearson.

McLaughlin, M. (2012). *Guided comprehension for English learners.* Newark, DE: International Reading Association.

McLaughlin, M., and Overturf, B. J. (2013). *The Common Core: Graphic organizers for teaching K–12 students to meet the Reading Standards.* Newark, DE: International Reading Association.

Serafini, F., and Blasingame, J. (2012). The changing face of the novel. *The Reading Teacher, 66*(2), 145–48.

YOUNG ADULT BOOKS CITED

Cheng, A. (2013). *Etched in clay: The life of Dave, enslaved potter and poet.* New York, NY: Lee & Low Books.

de Graaf, A. (2012). *Son of a gun.* Grand Rapids, MI: Eerdmans.

Doherty, B. (2008). *The girl who saw lions.* New York, NY: Roaring Brook Press.

Ellis, D. (2014). *The cat on the wall.* Toronto, ON: Groundwood.

Ellis, D. (2014). *Moon at nine.* Toronto, ON: Pajama Press.

Engle, M. (2014). *Silver people: Voices from the Panama Canal.* Boston, MA: Houghton Mifflin.

Hale, S. (2014). *Dangerous.* New York, NY: Bloomsbury.

Hartnett. S. (2011). *The midnight zoo.* Somerville, MA: Candlewick.

Herrick, S. (2009). *Cold skin.* Honesdale, PA: Front Street Press.

Hooper, M. (2008). *Newes from the dead.* New York, NY: Roaring Brook Press.

Mylnowski, S. (2014). *Don't even think about it.* New York, NY: Delacorte.

Myracle, L. (2014). *ttyl.* New York, NY: Abrams.

Myracle, L. (2014). *yolo.* New York, NY: Abrams.

Richards, J. (2010). *Three rivers rising: A novel of the Johnstown Flood.* New York, NY: Knopf Books for Young Readers.

Wiles, D. (2014). *Revolution.* New York, NY: Scholastic.

Wolf, A. (2011). *The watch that ends the night: Voices from the Titanic.* Somerville, MA: Candlewick Press.

Zusak, M. (2006). *The book thief.* New York, NY: Knopf.

Chapter Five

Anchoring the Teaching of Argumentative Writing Units with Young Adult Literature

Christian Z. Goering, Nikki Holland, and Sean P. Connors

In 2010, the Common Core State Standards ushered in a host of changes to the way reading and writing is taught in America's schools. Some of these changes were welcomed, such as a focus on fewer standards that purportedly raised the bar on the NCLB era of American education, one in which proficiency on checklists of competencies was championed as the way forward. Make no mistake, we also see a host of issues that come along with the new standards, and from the big picture of teaching and learning (Endacott and Goering, 2014) to text complexity (Connors and Shepard, 2012), the list of exemplars (Goering and Connors, 2014), and the return to close reading pedagogy (Connors and Rish, 2014).

The idea for this chapter began to germinate in the midst of a collaborative project between the University of Arkansas and the Berryville Public Schools vis-à-vis the College Ready Writers Program (CRWP). The initiative is a grant-funded subsidiary of Race to the Top Investing in Innovation (i3) funds, a local site of a national study undertaken by the National Writing Project.

The project seeks to help rural school districts implement informational and argumentative writing in its seventh through tenth grade English teachers' classrooms with hopes of seeing differences through a delayed random treatment comparison. The authors serve as principal investigators on the grant as well as part of the Northwest Arkansas Writing Project site leadership team at the University of Arkansas.

While we feel the work is important, we have also individually and collectively come to understand it as very difficult. Informally, the authors believe that most English teachers came to the profession primarily through a love of literature and passion for teaching literature, much more so than for the teaching of writing. What, for example, is a teacher's identity who enters the profession as a lover of literature and reading with the express goals of sharing those passions with her students? How does teacher identity impact one's ability to teach ideas, concepts, or with materials that fall outside of that identity?

Studies of the influence of teachers' identity show that epistemological beliefs about teaching and learning are the most important determinant of what is taught in the classroom and how (Langer and Applebee, 1987; Hillocks, 1999; Newell et al., 2014).

And herein rests part of the struggle: Teachers across the country are primarily prepared through literature-heavy English programs. The authors were prepared through similar programs and work with about a dozen new-to-the-profession teachers each year who have similar backgrounds.

An extrapolation of the twelve teachers in the authors' average MAT program will be used to represent the teaching population and thus, these teachers each graduated with degrees in English literature save one. Teaching writing is messy and difficult and time-consuming and for some, there's not near the rewards in helping a reluctant student labor through an argumentative essay as there is when a student's light bulb turns on from reading a work of literature. Teaching in a situation that is outside of how one identifies as a learner and a teacher may do more harm than good.

Our immersion in the work of helping teachers—most of whom see themselves first as literature teachers—make progress with their students in terms of argumentative writing has given us some insights on what works; more importantly, we've narrowed a common cause, to invoke the use of young adult literature as fulcrum texts for argumentative writing units of instruction, hereby advancing the teaching of YA while simultaneously meeting the demands of the CCSS to increase argumentative writing ability in students.

Anecdotally, we've each experienced schools in our area taking the exact wrong approach to responding to the instructional shifts necessary to help students meet the CCSS. From districts purchasing every single book on the list of exemplars to others interpreting the split between fiction and nonfiction (30/70 in high school) only in the context of what texts English teachers use, as if students never encounter texts of another ilk throughout the rest of the school day.

Sadly, we've also seen both insidious and blatant local attacks on the value of YA in the context of teaching and learning in a CCSS America. In a similar fashion, asking teachers to give up or put aside literature in favor of argument, asking them to change their identities, felt like an uphill losing battle.

ANCHORING INSTRUCTION

Our approach of anchoring instruction with a piece of literature is derived from Wessling, Lillage, and Van Kooten (2010), advancing the idea of layering context and texture texts—typically made up of more nonfiction—with a fulcrum text (see figure 5.1). We are quick to agree that "reading, especially complex reading, doesn't occur in isolation" (Wessling, Lillage, and Van Kooten, 2010, p. 24) but see the purpose of a longer fulcrum text to not only hold diverse concepts and ideas but also hold students' attention and push the joy factor. Wessling, Lillage, and Van Kooten (2010) narrow a fulcrum text as "the most complex and the work that comes before and after helps to tease out and maneuver its complexities" (p. 24), while we see the role of the shorter nonfiction texts as the most complex.

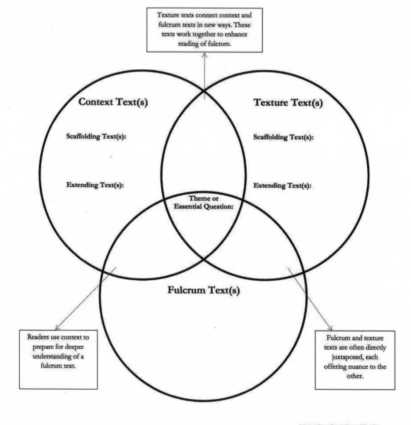

Adapted from Sarah Brown Wessling

Figure 5.1.

In thinking of a text to use to demonstrate these young adult literature anchored units, we thought immediately of John Corey Whaley's *Noggin*, the story of Travis Coates, a high school student who, after electing to die while facing a terminal illness, is reanimated five years later when his cryogenically frozen head is reattached to the body of another teenager. This text struck us as useful because it opened up several different potential themes for exploration through writing.

Euthanasia

In a sense, the reader experiences the aftermath and effects of Travis electing to die prior to the result of natural causes, a unique perspective. "Dying," Travis explains, "as it turns out, may not have been the best decision I ever made" (Whaley, 2014, p. 214).

Dystopia

The world Travis returns to, while normal, is anything but normal for him. His parents have secretly divorced. His former girlfriend is engaged. His best friend won't talk to him. He's back in his old high school, which, despite the five years, hasn't changed.

Isolation/Alienation

Travis is alone in a strange but familiar world. His best friend is living a lie about his sexuality. Another character says of the two of them, "Yeah. I mean, you're both living these lives you didn't choose to live with a world full of people telling you what that's supposed to mean" (Whaley, 2014, p. 104).

Celebrity

As a miracle of modern science, Travis has to learn to navigate the peculiar situation of his international celebrity, a task that is antithetical to his natural inclination not to be noticed. His experience gives us a rare glance into the insider's perspective of fame.

Illusion/Reality

The epigraph sets the stage for one of the most important topics: "It is just an illusion here on Earth that one moment follows another one, like beads on a string, and that once a moment is gone, it is gone forever" (Vonnegut quoted in Whaley, 2014).

Ethical Dilemmas in Science

Stem cells, cryogenics, organ donation, transplants—even if we could attach one person's head to another's body, should we? Transplanting an arm is one thing, a heart another, but what about a head, a brain, a person's identity? Where do we draw the line on alterations of the human body?

ARGUING THROUGH, ARGUING FROM *NOGGIN*

From the very beginning of our *Noggin* unit, we aim to get our students used to arguing and thinking critically about what they are reading while simultaneously finding joy in the class discussions and overall reading experiences. The goal for our students is to create meaning through multiple responses to literature (Rosenblatt, 1978), argumentation being one of the means of responding.

As the culminating writing assignment for our unit, we ask students to construct a literary analysis, taking a position on a controversy in the text using evidence from the novel and additional informational texts. In order to prepare them for this complex, dialogic writing task, we suggest a series of scaffolded experiences designed to help support their developing understanding of argument.

In "Best Practices in Teaching Argumentative Writing," Ferretti and Lewis (2013) define *argumentation* as "a verbal and social activity of reason aimed at increasing (or decreasing) the acceptability of a controversial standpoint for the listener or reader, by putting forward a constellation of propositions intended to justify (or refute) the standpoint before a rational judge" (p. 115).

To help our students develop an understanding of argument as involving a "constellation" of ideas, we focus in this unit on cultivating opportunities for dialogue about the novel and its related issues. Dialogue's importance to argument, particularly in the context of teaching students to write arguments, is well documented (Langer and Applebee, 1987; Morgan and Beaumont, 2003; Ferretti and Lewis, 2013). We hoped that creating opportunities for students to both talk with their peers and approach writing assignments from a dialogical perspective would help students to develop a more balanced perspective and enjoy the process of doing so.

As an introductory activity, we begin by reading students the first two pages of the novel, which set up the premise. We have included the first and last paragraph from that selection here:

Listen—I was alive once and then I wasn't. Simple as that. Now I'm alive again. The in-between part is still a little fuzzy, but I can tell you that, at some point or another, my head got chopped off and shoved into a freezer in Denver, Colorado.

. . .

I want to tell you a story about how you can suddenly wake up to find yourself living a life you were never supposed to live. It could happen to you, just like it happened to me, and you could try to get back the life you think you deserve to be living. Just like I did. (Whaley, 2013, pp. 1–2)

After students have time to write about and share their preliminary reactions to the text, we hand out the article "Head Transplants Are Coming Soon, at Least if This Doctor Gets His Way," which profiles a doctor who believes that the first head transplant operation could realistically come in as little as two years (Freeman, 2015). Once we have read that text out loud together, we invite students to mark up their copies, locating the main claim, highlighting the strongest evidence, and noting any information that is striking or interesting to them.

Once they have annotated the article, students return to their notebooks to consider what they want to know more about and where they stand on the issue now. Over the course of the next several class periods, while continuing our reading of *Noggin,* we present a "constellation" of ideas on the topic of head transplants with the goal of complicating students' thinking on the issue and introducing them to the practice of adjusting stance in response to new information.

To support students' digestion of the informational texts they encounter, we engage them in several more structured activities beyond the writing mentioned above. The primary goal of this series of activities is to continue to develop students' ability to integrate source material into their work. While learning to use sources is a practical skill for student writers, it's also an important barometer of their evolving understanding of academic writing as participation in a conversation.

Once students have had the opportunity to read several sources on a topic, we invite them to construct "They Say/I Say/Evidence" charts. In the "They Say" column on the left, students paraphrase the claims presented in the sources to which they hope to respond. In the "I Say" column, students write their response to the claim, and in the "Evidence" column, students cite evidence that supports their claim. Once students have constructed robust charts, they can translate those charts easily into an outline for their argument.

After outlining their arguments, students still need support in integrating source material. Beyond instruction in the basics such as evaluating evidence and summarizing sources, we focus attention on helping students to get the most out of the source material they bring in. First, we teach an adapted version of a "Say/Mean/Matter" chart, which asks students to respond to three questions: (1) What does it say? (2) What does it mean? and (3) Why does it matter? (Gallagher, 2013).

For each of the quotations they choose, we ask them to make a "quote sandwich" with the original source material at the top, followed by a statement about what they think the chosen material means, and closed with their thoughts on why this point is significant. Through this activity, students are learning to write warrants, which exposes their thinking and helps readers to see the connection between the source and the student's claim.

As a final preface to their culminating assignment, students learn about the moves that writers make with texts through Harris's (2006) approach. With middle and high school students, we focus on the four main moves that Harris articulates—to illustrate, to authorize, to extend, and to counter—which help students to think about different ways that source material can be used to support a point. In class, students review one another's essays, noting the moves that have been made in a particular piece and making an effort to be dexterous in the way that they employ the material.

Once students have made their way through this process as a class, we loosen the reins as much as possible and invite the students to dig deeply into the novel in the areas that are the most interesting to them. Their experience grappling with the central question of head transplants prepares them for independent work with another theme from the novel. *Noggin* raises many compelling topics: from ethical dilemmas surrounding issues such as euthanasia and cryogenics, to more personal questions related to identity, alienation, celebrity, and reality.

We designed our final project (see textbox 5.1) to give students as much autonomy to choose a topic of interest to them as possible, but also to provide some support and guidance as they embark on an inquiry-driven argument

---

TEXTBOX 5.1: FINAL WRITING ASSIGNMENT

Choose a selection from the book that raises an interesting question. What is that question? Using evidence from the novel and from additional informational sources, write an argument that attempts to answer that question. Once you have conducted your research and composed your argument, consider how your new understanding helps you to make sense of a central theme or character in the book. Be sure to use what you have learned about citing and quoting sources in your writing.

assignment, the process of which is likely unfamiliar for most students within the context of school. This assignment is an adaptation of Newkirk's (2014) "stories of our thinking," which he presents as a structure for literary analysis papers, and which we adapt to suit the task of argumentation.

So, for example, students might choose to write about a scene such as this one, in which Travis and his friend Hatton are discussing a show on TV that had been reporting on Travis's procedure:

> I was watching this show the other night. . . . And they were talking all about you. . . . And the reporter guy, you know the one with the weird name? He was asking them if they thought it was right. Not if they thought it was good for science or anything like that, but on a *personal* level, if they thought that bringing people back from the dead or whatever was right. If they thought it was okay. (Whaley, 2013, p. 103)

There are several questions being posed here: Are head transplants ethical? Is it up to individuals to decide on the conditions of their own death? Where do we draw the line when it comes to altering the human body? Students would choose the question that interests them most, curate a set of nonfiction sources that will help them take a position on the issue, and write an argument. Finally, they would consider how their newly informed position on the issue helps them to understand the novel.

Though this assignment would be most appropriate for upper-level students, it could easily be scaffolded for younger students. For example, teachers could invite all students to write about one quotation, or they could create a list of significant quotations from which students could choose. Teachers could also construct text sets themselves, either one central set for all students or a small selection of sets from which students could choose.

While we know that student motivation and writing achievement improves when students are invited to choose their own topics (Beers, 2013; Newell et al., 2011; Rathunde and Csikszentmihalyi, 2005), younger students especially may need the additional structure to help them identify the most salient issues in the novel and choose informational texts that complement one another and will help them answer their question.

DISCUSSION

Too often, literary analysis and argumentation are pitted against each other, competing for time in the English language arts classroom. We suggest, however, that these two purposes—to analyze and to persuade—complement one another and are particularly well suited to young adult literature. When teachers who identify as literature teachers feel pressured to teach argument, or any strategy or topic that doesn't map onto their vision of themselves as teachers for that matter, what often results is failure. Even ready-made activities are exceedingly difficult to implement when not fully understood or even accepted (Langer and Applebee, 1987, p. 67).

To many teachers, argument sounds adversarial, as they worry about trying to maintain "conflict-free zones" (Newell, Beach, Smith, and Vanderheide, 2014, p. 277). By bringing literature to the table, we are more likely to situate ourselves in a teacher's zone of proximal development. While some of the work in argument may be less comfortable, pairing the teaching of argument with the more familiar and fulfilling activities of reading and analyzing a novel make the experience much more likely to be successful.

In addition, the use of young adult literature in particular as the fulcrum text for an argumentative unit has the power to engage students in ways that both traditional literary analysis and traditional argument units may have struggled. When students are given the opportunity to immerse themselves in a story and think critically about what the text can help them understand about the world and their place in it, engagement and growth become more tangible.

In this unit and in our teaching more generally, we want students to think and write critically about texts, but we also want them to lose themselves in a novel for the pure aesthetic pleasure of doing so. We want to provide the structure and support that will help students to practice new skills in writing and reading, but we also want to give them the freedom that they so desperately need to explore the issues that are intriguing and meaningful to them. Giving students access to young adult literature and creating the space and support for them to engage in meaningful dialogue about that literature is one way to accomplish these goals.

REFERENCES

Beers, K. (2013). What matters most. *Journal of Adolescent & Adult Literacy, 57*(4), 265–69.

Connors, S. P., and Rish, R. (2014). Puzzle solving and modding: Two metaphors for examining the politics of close reading. *Reader, 67*, 94–118.

Connors, S. P., and Shepard, I. (2011/2012). Reframing arguments for teaching YA literature in an age of Common Core. *SIGNAL Journal, 35*(3), 6–10.

Endacott, J., and Goering, C. Z. (2014). Reclaiming the conversation on education. *English Journal, 103*(5), 89–92.

Ferretti, R. P., and Lewis, W. E. (2013). Best practices in teaching argumentative writing. In S. Graham, C. A. MacArthur, and J. Fitzgerald (eds.), *Best practices in writing instruction*, 2nd ed. (pp. 113–40).

Freeman, D. (2015, February 27). Head transplants are coming soon, at least if this doctor gets his way. Retrieved February 28, 2015.

Gallagher, K. (2004). *Deeper reading: Comprehending challenging texts, 4–12*. Portland, ME: Stenhouse.

Goering, C. Z., and Connors, S. P. (2014). Exemplars and epitaphs: Defending young adult literature. *Talking Points, 25*(2), 15–21.

Harris, J. (2006). *Rewriting how to do things with texts*. Logan, UT: Utah State University Press.

Hillocks, G., and Shulman, L. (1999). *Ways of thinking, ways of teaching*. New York: Teachers College Press.

Langer, J., and Applebee, A. (1987). *How writing shapes thinking: A study of teaching and learning*. Urbana, IL: National Council of Teachers of English.

Morgan, W., and Beaumont, G. (2003). A dialogic approach to argumentation: Using a chat room to develop early adolescent students' argumentative writing. *Journal of Adolescent & Adult Literacy, 47*(2), 146–57.

Newell, G. E., Beach, R., Smith, J., and Vanderheide, J. (2011). Teaching and learning argumentative reading and writing: A review of research. *Reading Research Quarterly, 46*(3), 273–304.

Newkirk, T. (2014). *Minds made for stories: How we really read and write informational and persuasive texts*. Portsmouth, NH: Heinemann.

Rathunde, K., and Csikszentmihalyi, M. (2005). Middle school students' motivation and quality of experience: A comparison of Montessori and traditional school environments. *American Journal of Education, 111*(3), 341–71.

Wessling, S. B., Lillge, D., and VanKooten, C. (2011). *Supporting students in a time of core standards: English language arts, grades 9–12*. Urbana, IL: National Council of Teachers of English.

Chapter Six

Using Young Adult Literature in Implementing Common Core Literacy Standards with Inclusion Students in Non-IDEA Classrooms

Lisa A. Hazlett and William Sweeney

Beginning in 1990 with the reauthorization of the Individuals with Disabilities Education Act (i.e., IDEA), this federal law protecting the educational rights for individuals with disabilities began to significantly emphasize the importance of academic performance in educational programs for students enrolled in special education courses (Yell, Ryan, Rozalski, and Katsiyannis, 2009). This academic focus continued gaining importance in the 1990s with pushes in inclusive programs, a greater emphasis on general education teachers' participation in the development and implementation of individual education programs, and greater emphasis on empirically driven curriculum, strategies, and daily monitoring approaches to assure appropriateness of educational programming for students exhibiting special needs characteristics (Fuchs and Fuchs, 2005; Fuchs, Fuchs, and Holleneck, 2007). This academic orientation, versus a tradition of functional and basic skills instruction, escalated further with the 2004 reauthorization of the Individuals with Disabilities Educational Improvement Act (Yell, 2012) in attempting to align IDEA with the reauthorization of the Elementary and Secondary School Act of 2001, that is, the No Child Left Behind Act (NCLB).

These endeavors to bring more philosophical, conceptual, and practical continuity to federal initiatives comprised efforts to assure highly qualified teachers and include all students in schoolwide assessment efforts to confirm sufficient annual yearly progress. Efforts to close the academic achievement gap for students, such as those with disabilities or other diverse backgrounds traditionally scoring significantly lower on academic achievement measures in reading and math, were added (Coyne, Kane"ennui, and Carnine, 2011).

These federal law changes related to accountability and empirically driven curriculums for students with disabilities are understandable, considering over two-thirds of students with disabilities spend the majority of their school day in general education settings (Heward, 2013). Although approximately 12 percent of public school students have disabilities, 90 percent of them spend some, if not most, of their time in general education classrooms. The largest single category of educational disabilities is Specific Learning Disabilities, including those identified with some form of a learning disability, with approximately 42.3 percent of all students with disabilities in this group (U.S. Department of Education, 2011).

Students with learning disabilities, combined with others exhibiting emotional and behavior disorders, speech and language difficulties, mild cognitive disabilities, and numerous other health impairments, comprise what is classified as High Incidence Disabilities that are typically found in many, if not most, general education classrooms across the country.

While inclusion students in traditional English language arts (ELA) classrooms are to pursue their peers' curriculum while also under IDEA's auspices, apprehensions follow regarding their peers and educators. Educator willingness and ability to suitably adapt course work is a necessity, as those with disabilities experience difficulties when activities are not differentiated to address their individual learning needs (McLeskey, Rosenberg, and Westling, 2010). Such unaddressed concerns would severely influence inclusion students' ability to assimilate and function effectively after high school (Heron and Harris, 1992), a central Common Core State Standards Initiative (2010) (CCSS) goal.

Although inclusion students tend to look, act, and socialize similarly to their same age and grade peers (Artiles, Harris-Murri, Rostenberg, 2006; McLeskey and Waldron, 2011; Taylor, 2005), Cole et al. (2004) found they often make greater gains academically and socially when included in general education classrooms rather than more restrictive settings. Stainback and Stainback (1996) readily acknowledge that acceptance, a mutual sense of belonging, and an environment that engenders reciprocal support, appreciation, and sensitivity to students' individual needs is often only a laudable goal rather than a reality within schools.

For example, students receiving inclusionary services in both general education classrooms and special education settings are somewhat separated from both peer sets, increasing unfamiliarity. Conflicts might occur between IDEA students attending traditional classrooms and those who do not; status hierarchies may form and create situations where inclusion students are as uncomfortable or stigmatized in IDEA classrooms as in non-IDEA ones (Heward, 2013).

Admittedly, creating positive classroom climates accentuating respect for all students can be challenging, as adolescence is a confusing period for all teens. However, inclusion teens' maturation may further isolate them by halting previous social activities. This group may have formed friendships with non-IDEA peers in elementary school, but then they are suddenly not invited to high school dances, games, or even selected for group work, all disconcerting and painful changes.

Frankly discussing inclusion students' general or individual concerns in secondary classrooms is difficult and irregularly addressed, if at all. Still, they are in these classrooms, and the above information is a compelling call for responsible consideration. The current question is, how can secondary ELA educators productively implement the CCSS with inclusion and non-inclusion students, producing genuine learning without stigmatization?

USING YAL

Young adult literature (YAL) is defined here as those works written *specifically for* adolescents aged 12 to 18, in grades 6 and 7 through 12. Numerous authors (e.g., Bushman and Bushman, 1994; Bushman and Haas, 2006; Herz and Gallo, 2005; Blasingame, 2007; Nilsen and Donelson, 2009; Cole, 2009) emphasize that YAL contains the same literary elements (consistent point of view, meaningful settings/themes, clear plotlines, vivid description, authentic dialogue, appealing style) as adult canonical works, but it is written commensurate with students' varied reading levels and sophistication for understanding and enjoyment.

Aside from YAL's literary content being more accessible to adolescents, of equal importance is its featuring characters and issues with which readers can readily relate, presented in a way that "does not invalidate, minimize, or devalue them" (p. 12), as stated by Blasingame (2007). Campbell (2000) shared the importance of YAL assisting adolescents' sense of self and identity:

> The central theme of most YA fiction is becoming an adult, finding the answer to the question "Who am I and what am I going to do about it?" No matter what events are going on in the book, accomplishing that task is really what the book is about, and in the climactic moment the resolution of the external conflict is linked to a realization for the protagonist that helps shape an adult identity. (p. 485)

Cart (2009) relayed the value of *all* readers seeing themselves in YAL titles, and receiving reassurance that their personal situations are not unique, but shared, managed, and overcome by many. Further emphasized was the importance of readers seeing others *different* from them, ultimately understanding that we are all part of humankind:

> Teenagers urgently need books that speak with relevance and immediacy to their real lives and to their unique emotional, intellectual, and developmental needs and that provide a place of commonality of experiences and mutual understanding. . . . By acquiring readers with the glorious varieties of the human experience, [YAL] invests young hearts and minds with tolerance, understanding, empathy, acceptance, compassion, kindness, and more. It civilizes them . . . and . . . I believe no other genre or literary form is as important. (p. 5)

Using literature portraying inclusion students as productive, independent, and confident role models in contemporary settings is a constructive method to acquire anticipated goals of encouraging cognizance, warmth, and acceptance of individual differences while tackling many of the most significant issues regarding peer and social rejection.

Carefully selected YAL works can assist in easing reservations and worries caused by unfamiliarity, thus replacing adverse views with knowledge and facts. Those YAL works featuring the chaotic adolescent years provide ways for inclusion and non-inclusion students to realize their commonalities, rather than emphasizing differences.

Essentially, by using YAL, students can understand, discuss, posit analyses and critiques, and use past material as these works meet their cognitive, experiential, emotional, and developmental levels; additionally, these skills are continually honed, ultimately creating students' sophisticated literacy skills and lifelong reading.

PROFESSIONAL ACCREDITATION AND SUPPORT FOR YAL

Professional organizations for the ELA, reading, and library sciences have long supported YAL, and additionally offer memberships in YAL sub-groups with accompanying journals, information, and resources. Young adult literature's importance is affirmed by the National Council for Accreditation of Teacher Education (NCATE) (currently transforming to the Council for the Accreditation of Educator Preparation, or CAEP, with publications still titled NCATE), an accreditation agency for post-secondary institutions offering secondary (grades 7 through 12) ELA teacher preparation programs. Educator preparation providers seeking accreditation must adhere to the 2012

NCTE/NCATE ELA standards, with its Standard 1, Element 1 requiring that students demonstrate knowledge of and uses for YAL:

> Standard I: Candidates demonstrate knowledge of [ELA] . . . content that specifically includes . . . knowledge of the nature of adolescents as readers.
>
> Element 1: Candidates are knowledgeable about texts . . . including young adult. . . . They are able to use literary theories to interpret and critique a range of texts. (p. 1)

Although NCATE is the nation's largest accrediting organization, not all institutions use it, although pre-service ELA programs without YAL instruction are doubtless rare.

Inclusion students' position in ELA classrooms is tenuous; although their educational programs are covered under IDEA, as learners in so-called regular classes they are also expected to meet these rooms' various content requirements, including applicable standards. Depending upon their school, students may have a special education coordinator working with the classroom teacher to set their curriculum and incorporate or modify ELA concepts, which implies they are incapable of learning the content without additional assistance. Likewise, their expected adherence to standards, including the 2010 CCSS, would presumably be commensurate with their classroom situation.

Neither the NCTE/IRA ELA nor NCTE/NCATE standards specifically mention disabled/inclusion students, but presumably all standards for schools have variations of "all students can learn/meeting the needs of all students" statements, seemingly including this group.

CCSS FOR THE ENGLISH LANGUAGE ARTS AND INCLUSION STUDENTS

The CCSS for ELA appear contradictory regarding regular and inclusion students, as its language seems to both separate and share expectations for both groups. The core ELA goal is

> to create the next generation of K–12 standards in order to help ensure that all students are college and career ready in literacy no later than the end of high school. (p. 3)

Further, the CCSS's rigorous expectations for its Reading Standards for Literature 6–12 state, in part:

Rigor is also infused through the requirement that students read increasingly complex texts through the grades. Students advancing through the grades are expected to meet each year's grade-specific standards and retain or further develop skills and understandings mastered in preceding grades. (p. 36)

The CCSS address disability/inclusion students, but its short mission statement includes language similar to non-IDEA ones:

- "[(IDEA) students]—must be challenged to excel within the general curriculum and be prepared for success in their post-school lives, including college and/or careers" (p. 1). Further,
- "Students with disabilities [have] disabling conditions that significantly hinder their abilities to benefit from general education (IDEA 34 CFR §300.39, 2004). Therefore, *how* these high standards are taught and assessed is of the utmost importance" (p. 1).

While acknowledging IDEA and students' limitations, the CCSS also call for increased performance *within the general curriculum*, and imply changed instructional techniques will reduce or eliminate the curricular modifications necessary for many to join non-IDEA rooms. Presumably, IDEA students are to be transformed into non-IDEA ones, with their school experience culminating in readiness for post-secondary education and careers. These are desired goals, but its assumed applicability to all appears too ambitious. Inclusion students are in non-IDEA classrooms because they receive assistance and should not be considered as lower level or lesser motivated. Further, the CCSS section "What Is Not Covered by the Standards" includes another IDEA-based statement, which reads in part:

It is also beyond the scope of the Standards to define the full range of supports appropriate for . . . students with special needs. . . . All students must have the opportunity to learn and meet the same high standards if they are to access the knowledge and skills necessary in their post–high school lives. (p. 6)

While this is another desired goal, it is also an ambitious implication of IDEA assistance and influence lessening in order for IDEA-students' higher classroom achievement and subsequent success.

Regardless, state education departments other than AL, MN (has adopted ELA standards only), NE, OK, TX, VA, and Puerto Rico have adopted the CCSS (CCSS, 2015) for implementation by public school educators and post-secondary pre-service students. Previous state standards presented objectives separately or in small themed groupings, such as this Grade 10 Listening, Viewing, and Speaking set, addressing oral presentation evaluation:

- 10.LVS.1.1 Students can analyze visual and auditory impact on the credibility and reliability of the message.
- 10.LVS.1.2 Students can evaluate the effectiveness of arguments used by speakers.
- 10.LVS.1.3 Students can analyze how verbal and nonverbal communication can influence the interpretation of the message. (South Dakota Department of Education, 2007)

The CCSS version of the above reads:

- Speaking and Listening Standards, Grades 9–10 students:

  3. Evaluate a speaker's point of view, reasoning, and use of evidence and rhetoric, identifying any fallacious reasoning or exaggerated or distorted evidence. (CCSS, p. 50)

Previous core ELA goals and objectives remain in the CCSS, but condensing standards presents fewer, yet far broader, ones, and creates more ambiguous interpretations. The CCSS for the ELA show grades 6–8, 9–10, and 11–12 each having a separate set of ten standards for literature (fiction), informational text (nonfiction), and writing. The sets for speaking and listening and language contain six standards each, with the standards themselves covering seventeen pages of text.

The plethora of recently published books serving to explain, simplify, and otherwise clarify the CCSS are flooding the market, but Burke's 2013 texts *The Common Core Companion: The Standards Decoded, Grades 6–8* and *The Common Core Companion: The Standards Decoded, Grades 9–12*, at 252 and 236 pages respectively, perhaps best demonstrate the challenges they are presenting to ELA educators.

CCSS AND YAL FOR THE ENGLISH LANGUAGE ARTS

The CCSS will either be YAL's greatest *proponent* or *opponent* in classrooms based upon the interpretation of its goal of producing students who are "college and career ready" (p. 3). Unfortunately, YAL's reputation and classroom use before the CCSS, regardless of quality, suitability, professional interest and promotion, or accreditation requirement, was ambivalent.

YAL's strongest opponent is the traditional classics (defined here as literature written by and for adults of past centuries), which remain the most commonly taught ELA texts (Bull, 2011, pp. 61–62). Numerous educators and researchers working with YAL agree, including Bushman and Bushman, 1994; Gallo, 2001; Applebee, Langer, Nystrand, Gamoran, and Martin, 2003; Bean and Harper, 2004; Claiborne, 2004; Herz and Gallo, 2005; and Bushman and Haas, 2006.

There are many reasons for canonical rule, but ELA educators generally consider YAL of lower quality, meant for younger or lower-level students; indeed, NCTEs membership reports 35,000, but ALANs is approximately 1,500 with its yearly workshop attendance 350 (T. Lesesne, personal communication, July 9, 2014).

As the classics are predominately taught, they are the titles available and retain continuity; one teaches like colleagues, using what is in the curriculum, in anthologies, and on shelves. Parents, administrators, and society expect both classics and ELA programs to prepare future educators for them; pre-service students are guaranteed only one YAL course (but not its quality) if from an NCTE/NCATE-accredited program.

In one's worst interpretation of the CCSS's view of YAL, one fears a reaping of the few titles currently used, replaced by canonical classics and other adult-level works. This is supported by the CCSS's suggested readings; only some (and dated) YAL is cited with its core reading list appearing sophisticated, unappealing, and rather esoteric. Some examples include Alcott's 1869 *Little Women,* Cooper's 1973 *The Dark Is Rising* (YAL), Churchill's 1940 Parliament Address, and Petry's 1955 *Harriet Tubman: Conductor on the Underground Railroad* (CCSS, 2010).

However, another interpretation of the CCSS shows YAL at their core. Remembering the qualities and purposes of YAL as previously presented, it is difficult imagining them *not* used for attaining goals set. The 2006 ACT report titled *Reading Between the Lines: What the ACT Reveals about College Readiness in Reading* states:

> The clearest differentiator in reading between students who are college ready and students who are not is the ability to comprehend complex texts. (p. 2)

Similarly, Allyn (2013) concludes:

> A disastrous outcome of the [CCSS] would be to implement them solely through a list of wonderful but deeply challenging texts at each grade level and teach solely and exclusively to those texts without giving our students the necessary foundational skills to successfully do so. We must use those texts and other less complex texts to teach the skills that will enable students to comprehend the complex texts on their own. (p. 28)

Aside from the above research citing YAL's importance to students' textual comprehension, others (Richardson, Morgan, and Fleener, 2012;

Allington, 2012; Ehri, Dreyer, Flugman, and Gross, 2007) specified all students need texts they can read and understand (i.e., at their appropriate level) to significantly improve reading skills.

A goal of both YAL and the CCSS is to produce lifelong readers, and Allyn (2013) reminds us that students must be able to read texts in their original form; in other words, commercial or Internet study guides are unnecessary if the work is on the students' level. Allyn later continues:

> [this also denies] the opportunity to think deeply about the meanings behind [texts] and to apply them to their lives. Offering...texts that are too simplified or too complex is unrealistic and doesn't reflect the real world of a reader. (p. 43)

Selecting appropriate texts requires that educators use their own professional judgment rather than relying upon supplied works, and match readers to texts/purposes. Educators must thus read more, and from a wider variety of titles (including YAL), which should also force acknowledgment that the canon cannot meet all needs. Again, how schools *interpret* the CCSS will determine efficacy.

PURPOSES OF INCLUSION-THEMED YAL

As teaching adult canonical works poses difficulties for non-IDEA students, inclusion students will doubtless find them doubly challenging. The benefits of YAL for non-inclusion students also apply to inclusion ones, but ideally they would also reflect inclusion students' personal struggles through like protagonists and situations. Further, if non-inclusion students had opportunities to read about those unlike themselves, this could initiate a classroom climate reflecting openness and belonging among all students.

Indeed, Michael Cart asserted in *Necessary Noise* (2003) that schools' attempts at integrating non-majority students remain largely ineffective, resulting in continued invisibility, patronization, bullying, or other stigmatizations by majority peers. It is vital that majority adolescents learn of the often-radical dissimilarities that comprise their peers' daily lives. Cart states:

> Kids need to learn empathy. They need to learn how the *other* can become *us*. (p. x)
>
> [A suggested method] is through reading fiction that captures—artfully, authentically, and unsparingly—the circumstances of kids [who are non-majority]. (p. xiii)

Newer exceptionality titles focus more upon chronic illnesses and conditions (e.g., cancer, depression, weight) than intellectual disabilities, with fewer still featuring inclusion situations. Although exposure to such YAL is beneficial to all, considering IDEA students' various issues is difficult when novels are scarce.

EXAMPLES OF INCLUSION-THEMED YAL

Still, YAL offers titles portraying intellectually challenged protagonists, albeit to differing degrees. Jack Gantos's Joey Pigza, an irrepressible teen battling severe emotional and behavior disorders, is featured in four humorous novels, beginning with *Joey Pigza Swallowed the Key* (2001), all for middle grades students. Similarly themed are Brent Crawford's three titles featuring freshman Will Carter; *Carter Finally Gets It* (2009) begins the series.

Autism spectrum disorders (and formerly Asperger's syndrome) exhibit numerous titles, including Beverly Brenna's *Wild Orchard* (2005) and sequel, *Waiting for No One* (2011), portraying an eighteen-year-old female moving beyond her sheltered world. Likewise, Tara Kelly's *Harmonic Feedback* (2010) and Francisco X. Stork's *Marcelo in the Real World* (2009) feature Asperger's, showing protagonists handling new challenges and discovering satisfying lives. Another pairing is Anna Kerz's *The Mealworm Diaries* (2009) and *Better Than Weird* (2011) featuring socially awkward Aaron.

Herb Helman's *Running on Dreams* (2007) presents Justin, beginning his first semester in a mainstream school, and Jude Welton's *Adam's Alternative Sports Day* (2005) shows nine-year-old Adam learning to compete with peers. Finally, Stasia Ward Kehoe's *The Sound of Letting Go* (2014) features Daisy, navigating high school and life with her autistic, violent brother. Especially well-written, this dares to show autism's darker aspects.

Various disabilities appear in Don Gallo's short story collection *Owning It: Stories about Teens with Disabilities* (2008); likewise, Don Trembath's *Rooster* (2005) has a high school male supervising a special needs adult bowling team. In K. A. Nuzum's *A Small White Scar* (2006) fifteen-year-old Will leaves home to become a cowboy, unaware that his intellectually disabled brother has followed him.

Although older, Rodman Philbrick's *Freak the Mighty* (1993) portrays a touching friendship between a mentally challenged boy and one with physical disabilities; his later *Max the Mighty* (1998) shows Max drawing upon his now-deceased friend's strength to assist an abused girl.

Cerebral palsy is more frequent; Harriet McBryde Johnson's *Accidents of Nature* (2007) features seventeen-year-old Jean working at a summer camp for disabled children, and Cammie McGovern's *Say What You Will* (2014) follows an isolated senior who uses a computer to speak. Ron Koertge's *Stoner and Spaz* (2002) and *Now Playing: Stoner and Spaz II* (2011) humorously follow a boy with cerebral palsy and his drug-addicted female friend; likewise, Terry Trueman's unforgettable *Stuck in Neutral* (2000) and sequel *Life Happens Next* (2012) follow fourteen-year-old Shawn, unable to communicate with the outside world while sharing his genius IQ with readers. Another tragic story is Ben Mikaelsen's *Petey* (1998), shown as an adult whose cerebral palsy was misdiagnosed when he was a child.

Once fairly popular, there are few contemporary titles featuring Down syndrome. Regardless of date, nearly all are stereotyped and typically portray hulking, tantrum-prone secondary male characters feared or taunted.

Titles with traumatic brain injuries (TMI) are increasingly popular, with most impairment from athletics. While *acquired* and essentially preventable, TMIs are not congenital and characters work to return to their former abilities, unavailable to those born with intellectual disabilities. Interestingly, these characters resembled traditional readers until incurring their disability; only a few tragic seconds separate them. Protagonists' new and unforeseen lifestyle restrictions, as well as friendship and relationship losses and changes, strongly illustrate unforgiving realities and how not to treat others. When characters begin successfully living *with* and accepting their situation rather than withdrawing or railing *against* it, discussion can center on learned lifestyle skills and techniques, illustrating to all how lives can proceed differently than planned, yet successfully. Novels featuring TMIs include Ben Mikaelsen's *Touching Spirit Bear* (2004), *Open Ice* by Pat Hughes (2005), Susan Vaught's *Trigger* (2006), Kerry Madden's *Louisiana Song* (2007), and Nancy Hartry's *Watching Jimmy* (2009). Older quality titles include Chris Crutcher's *The Crazy Horse Electric Game* (1987) and short story "Telephone Man" (1989), plus Alden Carter's *Dancing on Dark Water* (1990).

INCLUSION-THEMED NONFICTION YAL

Nonfiction, a separate and especially important CCSS category, features titles for students and parents. Autobiographies and memoirs offer camaraderie to those with similar issues, and are especially valuable regarding lesser-publicized and/or occurring disabilities, such as Samantha Abeel's *My Thirteenth Winter: A Memoir* (2003), depicting dyscalculia.

Informational books date quickly, but quality sources include Rowman & Littlefield's *The Ultimate Teen Guide Series*, which offers a variety of titles. One editor oversees the various individual authors, most having personal experience with its subject; an example is *Speech and Language Challenges: The Ultimate Teen Guide (It Happened to Me)* by Marlene Targ Bell (2014).

A similar series is *USA TODAY Health Reports*, published by Millbrook Press and located under their Twenty-First Century Books category; one example is *USA TODAY Health Reports: Diseases and Disorders (Anxiety Disorders)* by Cherry Pedrick and Bruce Hyman (2012). Anticipating CCSS, each title identifies its Lexile Level in addition to regular ratings.

Of course, inclusion students need more than titles focusing on disabilities. Aside from regular YAL, Orca Publishing offers an impressive series of shorter fiction and nonfiction for struggling elementary through high school readers, with over five hundred titles available and approximately sixty-five published annually. Titles are meant to be read in one or two sittings and focus on contemporary children/teens and their various issues (Orca Publishing, 2014). A secondary example is *Above All Else* (2014) by Jeff Ross, which follows a protagonist searching for the person who injured his friend during a high-stakes soccer game.

USING YAL WITH INCLUSION STUDENTS

Aside from utilizing effective teaching, additional suggestions for the successful utilization of inclusion-themed YAL are below.

- Titles must be of quality and relay universal adolescent experiences.
- Center classroom discussion on the novel's plot, as targeting disabilities separates students from characters and perpetuates stereotypes. Instead, familiar teaching techniques enable inclusive, meaningful discussion.
- Ask, "Where/how do *you* fit into the story?" Readers can vicariously identify with fantastical characters, situations, or other literary inventions, so this question helps non-inclusion students empathize with disabled characters' situations and issues.
- Intersperse titles throughout the curriculum, rather than one unit with multiple works. Reading these titles with others will accustom students to their themes, diminishing stigmas.
- Never presume students are uninterested in a work because its subject appears unrelated to their lives. Time travel, murderous mermaids, or becoming zombies are hardly experienced, but do not preclude reading pleasure.
- Resist designating inclusion students as class spokespersons for their disability, as repeatedly hearing one voice produces the assumption all students with this issue are alike. Regardless, students should never be expected to discuss personal matters.

- Recommend a variety of works to inclusion students rather than only disability-themed ones; all students have favorite genres and subjects and should be encouraged to read from a variety of works.
- Educators should be knowledgeable of the inclusion issue discussed, with current supplemental resources available.

USING YAL WITH INCLUSION AND LOWER-LEVEL STUDENTS

Beers's 1990 dissertation classifying adolescents' reading styles (e.g., Avid, Dormant, Uncommitted, Unmotivated, and Unskilled) and preferences (e.g., select own books versus choosing from small title set) has been continually enriched, with her 2003 text consistently cited by researchers, including ELAs Reid and Cline, 1997; Lesesne, 2006; Wilhelm, 2010; Martinez and Harmon, 2011; Manuel, 2012; and Donalson and Halsey, 2013.

As *inclusion* refers to *student placement* rather than specific disabilities or conditions, inclusion students' reading strengths and weaknesses are as varied as non-inclusion students'. However, struggling readers, and those generally disliking reading, can benefit from these suggestions regarding YAL's general use and presentation.

- Because this group reads relatively little, their reading skills are deficient, leading to viewing reading as onerous with difficulty beginning reading assignments. Reading part of the assigned work aloud while students follow the text allows them to begin the piece, with hearing pronunciation, pauses, expression, and so on, building skills.
- These students generally prefer other activities to reading, viewing it as unimportant or removed from their lives. However, nonfiction, photo-biographies, or other factual works are viewed as more relevant and interesting (Beers, 2003; Mercer, Mercer, and Pullen, 2011), so these should be emphasized.
- This group often views discussing titles as intangible and insignificant (Beers, 2003). However, completing novel-based activities (e.g., creating a collage) results in a product and should be encouraged as applicable.
- These readers find choosing novels from libraries especially difficult and confusing (Beers, 2003), as numerous titles are overwhelming. Less intimidating is pre-selecting books and allowing students to decide among them.

- Likewise, this group prefers reading books others recommend; if another enjoyed it, they should also (Beers, 2003). Students recommending titles and choosing books as above builds selection confidence.
- Due to the diversity of instructional needs of students with disabilities, teachers must provide additional guidance and differentiation. While these students should benefit from YAL, they may need alternative instructional strategies, such as guided notes (Sweeney, Ehrhardt, Gardner, Jones, Greenfield, and Fribley, 1999) or structured study guides (Lazarus, 1996), to augment the curriculum selected for instruction (Mercer et al., 2010).
- Finally, this group may enjoy a title, but once read not select another until assigned. Educators should note what students are reading, and provide another similarly themed novel of likely interest to assist them in reading continuity.

CONCLUSION

Although titles dealing with various inclusion situations (especially Down syndrome) are hardly prolific, their scarcity does serve to emphasize their absence; that is, it is clearly evident that many adolescents are still absent from YAL, positively or otherwise. However, as educators we can bemoan this only so much; if more novels are desired, then we must request them—or pen them ourselves.

Persistent absence from novels causes ELA classrooms to marginalize inclusion students in both school and society, while also creating a disservice to traditional students by allowing unneeded separations to continue. If not represented in literature and the classroom, those absent naturally receive negative messages regarding their self-esteem, self-worth, and future potential. Seemingly, those absent are omitted for a reason; surely the assumption is those missing are too unimportant or scarce to include, with such conclusions extending to non-IDEA students, as exclusions imply the same for all.

Of course, YAL with inclusion themes assists these students' perception, awareness, and acceptance of themselves, all necessary for meaningful and productive adult lives. Likewise, it is also important for traditional teens to read inclusion-themed YAL, as it will reinforce their recognition of commonalities shared and surely aid in more positive behaviors toward inclusion peers.

If honest and respectful discussion about these works is present, inclusion and traditional students should feel more comfortable promoting various conversations, interactions, and friendships with one another in school and afterward, which is a worthy goal; also firmly meeting the desired post-secondary success of the Common Core State Standards.

REFERENCES

Abeel, S. (2003). *My thirteenth winter: A memoir.* New York, NY: Scholastic.

ACT. (2006). *Reading between the lines: What the ACT reveals about college readiness in reading.* Retrieved June 1, 2014, from http://act.org/research/policymakers/pdf/reading_summary.pdf.

The ALAN Review. (2014). Retrieved from www.alan-ya.org.

Allington, D. (2012). Private experience, textual analysis, and institutional authority: The discursive practice of critical interpretation and its enactment in literary training. *Language and Practice, 21*(2), 211–15.

Allyn, P. (2013). *Be core ready.* Boston, MA: Pearson.

American Library Association. (2014). Retrieved from www.ala.org.

Applebee, A. N., Langer, J., Nystrand, M., Gamoran, M., and Martin, A. (2003). Discussion-based approaches to developing understanding: Classroom instruction and student performance in middle and high school English. *American Educational Research Journal, 40*(3), 685–730.

Artiles, A. J., Harris-Murri, N., and Rostenberg, D. (2006). Inclusion as social justice: Critical notes on discourses, assumptions, and the road ahead. *Theory Into Practice, 45*(3), 260–68.

Assembly on Literature for Adolescents of the NCTE ALAN Workshop. (2014). Retrieved from www.alan-ya.org.

Bean, T. W., and Harper, H. J. (2004). Teacher education and adolescent literacy. In T. L. Jetton, and J. A. Dole (eds.), *Adolescent literacy research and practice* (pp. 392–411). New York, NY: Guilford Press.

Beers, K. (1990). "Choosing not to read: An ethnographic study of seventh-grade aliterate students." Thesis (EdD), University of Houston.

Beers, K. (2003). *When kids can't read: What teachers can do.* Portsmouth, NH: Heinemann.

Bell, M. T. (2014). *Speech and language challenges: The ultimate teen guide (It happened to me).* Lanham, MD: Rowman & Littlefield.

Blasingame, J. (2007). *Books that don't bore 'em.* New York, NY: Scholastic.

Brenna, B. (2005). *Wild orchard.* Calgary, AB, Canada: Red Deer Press.

Brenna, B. (2011). *Waiting for no one.* Calgary, AB, Canada: Red Deer Press.

Bryan, T. (1997). Assessing the personal and social status of students with learning disabilities. *Learning Disabilities Research and Practice, 12,* 36–76.

Bull, K. B. (2011). Identifying obstacles and garnering support: Young adult literature in the English language arts classroom. In J. A. Hayn and J. S. Kaplan (eds.), *Teaching young adult literature today* (pp. 61–71). Lanham, MD: Rowman & Littlefield.

Burke, J. (2013). *The common core companion: The standards decoded, grades 6–8.* Thousand Oaks, CA: Corwin.

Burke, J. (2013). *The common core companion: The standards decoded, grades 9–12.* Thousand Oaks, CA: Corwin.

Bushman, J. B., and Haas, K. P. (2006). *Using young adult literature in the English classroom.* Upper Saddle River, NJ: Pearson/Merrill Prentice Hall.

Bushman, J. H., and Bushman, K. P. (1994). *Teaching English creatively.* Springfield, IL: Charles C. Thomas.

Campbell, P. (2000). The sand in the oyster: Middle muddle. *Horn Book 76* (July–August 2000), 483–85.

Cart, M. (2003). *Necessary noise: Stories about our families as they really are.* New York, NY: HarperCollins.

Cart, M., and Jenkins, C. A. (2006). *The heart has its reasons.* Lanham, MD: Scarecrow Press.

Carter, A. (1990). *Dancing on dark water.* New York, NY: Scholastic.

Claiborne, J. L. (2004). *A survey of high school English teachers to determine their knowledge, use, and attitude related to young adult literature in the classroom.* Unpublished doctoral dissertation, University of Tennessee, Knoxville.

Cole, P. B. (2009). *Young adult literature in the 21st century.* Boston, MA: McGraw-Hill.

Coyne, M. D., Kame"ennui, E. J., and Carnine, D. W. (eds.). (2011). *Effective teaching strategies that accommodate diverse learners* (4th ed.). Upper Saddle River, NJ: Pearson.

Crawford, B. (2009). *Carter finally gets it.* New York, NY: Hyperion.

Crutcher, C. (1987). *The crazy horse electric game.* New York, NY: HarperCollins.

Crutcher, C. (1989). "Telephone Man." In *Athletic shorts* (pp. 131–54). New York, NY: Delacorte.

Donalson, K., and Halsey, P. (2013). Adolescent readers' perceptions of remedial reading classes: A case study. *Reading Improvement, 50*(4), 189–98.

Ehri, L. C., Dreyer, L. G., Flugman, B., and Gross, A. (2007). Reading rescue: An effective tutoring intervention model for language-minority students who are struggling readers in first grade. *American Educational Research Journal, 44,* 414–48.

Fuchs, L. S., and Fuchs, D. (2005). Responsiveness-to-intervention: A blueprint for practitioners, policymakers, and parents. *Teaching Exceptional Children, 38*(1), 57–61.

Fuchs, L. S., and Fuchs, D. (2007). A model for implementing responsiveness to intervention. *Teaching Exceptional Children, 39*(5), 14–20.

Fuchs, L. S., Fuchs, D., and Hollenbeck, K. N. (2007). Extending responsiveness to intervention to mathematics at first and third grade. *Learning Disabilities Research and Practice, 22,* 13–24.

Gallo, D. (2001). How classics create an aliterate society. *English Journal, 90*(3), 33–39.

Gallo, D. (2008). *Owning it: Stories about teens with disabilities.* Somerville, MA: Candlewick.

Gantos, J. (2001). *Joey Pigza swallowed the key.* New York, NY: HarperCollins.

Hartry, N. (2009). *Watching Jimmy.* Toronto, ON, Canada: Tundra Books.

Heiman, H. (2007). *Running on dreams.* Shawnee Mission, KS: Autism Asperger's Publishing Company.

Heron, T. E., and Harris, K. C. (1992). *The educational consultant* (3rd ed.). Austin, TX: PRO-ED.

Herz, S. K., and Gallo, D. R. (2005). *From Hinton to Hamlet.* Westport, CT: Greenwood Press.

Heward, W. L. (2013). *Exceptional children* (10th ed.). Upper Saddle River, NJ: Pearson.

Hughes, P. (2005). *Open ice.* New York, NY: Delacorte.

Individuals with Disabilities Education Improvement Act of 2004, P.L. 108–446. (2014). Retrieved from www.parentcenterhub.org/respository/idea.

The International Reading Association. (2014). Retrieved from www.reading.org.

International Reading Association and the National Council of Teachers of English. (1996). *Standards for the English Language Arts.*

International Reading Association Special Interest Group: Network on Adolescent Literature. (2014). Retrieved from www.signal-ya.org.

Johnson, H. (2007). *Accidents of nature.* New York, NY: Henry Holt.

Journal of Adolescent & Adult Literacy. (2014). Retrieved from www.reading.org/general/Publications/Journals/JAAL.aspx.

Kehoe, S. (2014). *The sound of letting go.* New York, NY: Viking Penguin.

Kelly, T. (2010). *Harmonic feedback.* New York, NY: Henry Holt.

Kerz, A. (2009). *The mealworm diaries.* Victoria, BC, Canada: Orca.

Kerz, A. (2011). *Better than weird.* Victoria, BC, Canada: Orca.

Koertge, R. (2002). *Stoner and Spaz.* Somerville, MA: Candlewick.

Koertge, R. (2011). *Now playing: Stoner and Spaz II.* Somerville, MA: Candlewick.

Lazarus, B. D. (1996). Flexible skeletons: Guided notes for adolescents with mild disabilities. *Teaching Exceptional Children, 28*(3), 37–40.

Lesesne, T. (2006). *Naked reading.* Portland, ME: Stenhouse Publishers.

Madden, K. (2007). *Louisiana song.* New York, NY: Viking.

Manuel, J. (2012). Reading lives: Teenagers' reading practices and preferences. In J. Manuel and S. Brindley (eds.), *Teenagers and reading: Literary heritages, cultural contexts and contemporary reading practices* (pp. 12–37). Cambridge, MA: Wakefield Press.

Martinez, M. G., and Harmon, M. (2011). An investigation of student preferences of text formats. *The ALAN Review, 39*(1), 12–20.

McGovern, C. (2014). *Say what you will.* New York, NY: HarperTeen.

McLeskey, J., Rosenberg, M., and Westling, D. (2010). *Inclusion: Effective practices for all students.* Upper Saddle River, NJ: Pearson.

McLeskey, J., and Waldron, N. L. (2011). Educational programs for elementary students with learning disabilities: Can they be both effective and inclusive? *Learning Disabilities Research and Practice, 26*(1), 46–57.

Mercer, C. D., Mercer, A. R., and Pullen, P. C. (2011). *Teaching students with learning problems* (8th ed.). Upper Saddle River, NJ: Pearson.

Mikaelsen, B. (1998). *Petey.* New York, NY: Hyperion.

Mikaelsen, B. (2004). *Touching Spirit Bear.* New York, NY: HarperCollins.

Millbrook Press. (2014). Retrieved from www.lernerbooks.com/About-Lerner/pages/millbrook-press.aspx.

The National Council for Accreditation of Teacher Education. (2014). Retrieved from http://ncate.org/Public/AboutNCATE/QuickFacts/tabid/343/Default.aspx.

National Council of Teachers of English. (2014). Retrieved from www.ncte.org.

National Governors Association. (2010). *Common core state standards for English language arts and literacy in history/social studies, science, and technical subjects.* Washington, DC: NGA Center and CCSSO.

National Governors Association. (2015). *Standards in your state.* Washington, DC: NGA Center and CCSSO.

NCTE/NCATE Standards for Initial Preparation of Teachers of Secondary English Language Arts, Grades 7–12. (2012). Retrieved from www.ncte.org/library/NCTE Files/Groups/CEE/NCATE/ApprovedStandards_111212.pdf.

Nilsen, A. P., and Donelson, K. L. (2009). *Literature for today's young adults* (8th ed.). Boston, MA: Pearson Education, Inc.

Nuzum, K. A. (2006). *A small white scar.* New York, NY: HarperCollins.

Orca Publishing. (2014). Retrieved from www.orcabook.com.

Pedrick, C., and Hyman, B. (2012). *USA TODAY health reports: Diseases and disorders (Anxiety disorders).* Minneapolis, MN: Millbrook Press.

Philbrick, R. (1993). *Freak the mighty.* New York, NY: Scholastic.

Philbrick, R. (1998). *Max the mighty.* New York, NY: Scholastic.

Reed, L., and Cline, K. J. (1997). Our repressed reading addictions: Teachers and Young Adult Series Books. *English Journal, 86*(3), 68–72.

Richardson, J. S., Morgan, R. F., and Fleener, C. E. (2012). *Reading to learn in the content areas.* Belmont, CA: Wadsworth.

Ross, J. (2014). *Above all else.* Custer, WA: Orca.

SIGNAL Journal. (2014). Retrieved from www.signal-ya.org.

South Dakota Department of Public Education. (2007). *South Dakota Language Arts Content Standards.*

Stainback, S., and Stainback, W. (eds.). (1996). *Inclusion: A guide for educators* (2nd ed.). Baltimore, MD: Brooks.

Stork, F. X. (2009). *Marcelo in the real world.* New York, NY: Scholastic.

Sweeney, W. J., Ehrhardt, A. M., Gardner, R., Jones, L., Greenfield, R., and Fribley, S. (1999). Using guided notes with academically at-risk high school students during a remedial summer social studies class. *Psychology in the Schools, 36*(4), 305–18.

Tatum, A. (2008). Observed or underserved? A focus on adolescents and texts. *English Journal, 98*(2), 82–85.

Taylor, S. J. (2005). Caught in the continuum: A critical analysis of the principle of least restrictive environment. *Research and Practice for Persons with Severe Disabilities, 30,* 218–30.

Trembath, D. (2005). *Rooster.* Custer, WA: Orca.

Trueman, T. (2000). *Stuck in neutral.* New York, NY: HarperCollins.

Trueman, T. (2012). *Life happens next.* New York, NY: HarperCollins.

The Ultimate Teen Guide Series. (2014). Retrieved from www.scarecrowpress.com.

U.S. Department of Education. (2011). *Individuals with Disabilities Education Act (IDEA) data.* Washington, DC.

Vaught, S. (2006). *Trigger.* New York, NY: Bloomsbury.

Voice of Youth Advocates. (2014). Retrieved from www.voyamagazine.com.

Welton, J. (2005). *Adam's alternative sports day.* Philadelphia, PA: Jessica Kingsley.

Wilhelm, J. D. (2010). Literacy and neuroplasticity: Transforming our perspectives and ourselves. *Voices from the Middle, 17*(4), 37–40.

Yell, M. L. (2012). *The law and special education* (3rd ed.). Upper Saddle River, NJ: Pearson.

Yell, M. L., Ryan, J. B., Rozalski, M. E., and Katsiyannis, A. (2009). The U.S. Supreme Court and special education 2005 to 2007. *Teaching Exceptional Children, 41*(3), 68–75.

Young Adult Library Services. (2014). Retrieved from www.ala.org/yalsa.

Chapter Seven

Using Book Clubs and Adolescent Literature to Support the Common Core Standards

Jody Polleck

The Common Core State Standards (CCSS) have changed the way school districts nationwide are approaching instruction, assessment, and content, specifically within the discipline of English language arts. Because teachers are given little guidance as to "the how and the why," many educators are turning to prepackaged and state-developed curricula, where content makers have interpreted the CCSS in ways that are not meeting the needs of diverse students, particularly those living in urban areas whose identities and communities are not reflected in the CCSS materials.

In looking at the CCSS exemplar list (NGA, 2010), many of the texts are not relevant to students' lives or to their social-emotional development. While these texts are labeled as "suggested," many districts use them as prescriptions for their content. Specifically, within the list for grades 6 through 10, of the twenty-seven suggested texts, twenty are written by white authors. Further, only nine of the texts feature adolescent main characters and only seven were published within the last thirty years.

When we overrepresent the classics, which are mostly *about and for* adults, we are telling our students that their experiences have less value; simultaneously, we privilege canonical texts over the kinds of reading they do at home and within their communities (Ericson, 2001). Young adult literature (YAL) responds to our students' social, emotional, and cultural experiences in that it mirrors their challenges and struggles—a powerful tool for academic and social-emotional development (Coats, 2011).

In addition to suggesting texts that don't meet our students' needs, the CCSS has deemphasized our focus on literature overall. According to the

National Governors Association (2010), CCSS has a goal of students reading 70 percent informational texts and 30 percent literary texts. This certainly makes sense across *all* content areas, in that students should be reading in math, science, social studies, and technical subject areas (Moss, 2013).

This does not mean, however, that ELA teachers must shoulder the burden and change their curriculum to 70 percent informational text. In doing so, we privilege nonfiction over narrative and devalue fiction, poetry, and drama. This message implicitly tells our students that nonfiction is the only way to help them become "college and career ready."

The CCSS has also put strong emphasis on close readings, including the teaching of such skills as evidence citation and analysis (NGA, 2010). While I certainly am not arguing that these tasks are without value, I am arguing that close reading and "text-based answers" need to be balanced with aesthetic responses. If we ignore the pleasure associated with texts, then students are given an insular, one-sided purpose for reading. Reading becomes about information—and less about the connections they can make with the characters. Teaching students to love literature must come first—and must continue throughout adolescents' academic careers (Gibbons, Dail, and Stallworth, 2006).

Research around reading tells us that if students are *not* motivated to read, they will not read (Glaus, 2013; Henk, Marinak, and Melnick, 2013). Pre-scripted, canonical lists such as those in the CCSS are exactly the kinds of texts that will turn off many of our adolescents, particularly those who are struggling or reluctant (Glaus, 2013). Countless researchers and practitioners have demonstrated the power of YAL to help readers become more engaged while also employing rigorous analyses (Groenke and Scherff, 2010; Stallworth, 2006). The purpose of this chapter is to add to this body of research, illuminating how student-centered book clubs and YAL can be used to support CCSS in authentic, meaningful ways with self-selected, engaging texts.

RESEARCH AND THEORY ON YOUNG ADULT LITERATURE

Young adult literature is a powerful tool for *all* students: struggling and high-achieving, rural and urban, low- and high-income. YAL mirrors students' lives and takes into consideration their identity and development (Stallworth, 2006). Unfortunately, many educators and administrators choose not to use YAL for fear it is not as rich or rigorous as the canon.

Researchers have demonstrated the complexity and sophistication of YAL (Groenke and Scherff, 2010; Santoli and Wagner, 2004), as the genre has the quantitative demands that are required by the CCSS and rich vocabulary and figurative language (Ostenson and Wadham, 2012). In fact, if we are to use the CCSS quantitative tool for reading levels (Lexile), we can see that YAL is equal to the canon—and, in fact, exceeds much of the classics traditionally required for ELA classes. (See table 7.1.)

Table 7.1: Lexile Pairings of Texts

Text Pairings	Lexile Levels
Of Mice and Men (Steinbeck, 1937)	630L
Monster (Myers, 1999)	670L
Lord of the Flies (Golding, 1954)	770L
Tyrell (Booth, 2006)	780L
Huckleberry Finn (Twain, 1884)	990L
Watsons Go to Birmingham—1963 (Curtis, 2000)	1000L
Animal Farm (Orwell, 1945)	1170L
Curious Incident of the Dog in the Night-time (Haddon, 2003)	1180L
Romeo and Juliet (Shakespeare, 1597)	1260L
PunkZilla (Rapp, 2009)	1300L

These measurements demonstrate that YAL does contain the complexity that the CCSS requires. Because of its sophistication and challenge, YAL can develop students' reading skills while simultaneously enhancing their appreciation for literature.

THE POWER OF BOOK CLUBS

Book clubs have long traditions in the schools and beyond. In 2000, over 100,000 book clubs were in existence in the United States alone (Daniels, 2002). The popularity of these forums is due to the social act of reading, where participants share their experiences with literature and discuss how the texts connect to their own lives. Within these settings, readers use books and each other's responses to create shared interpretations of the texts and make powerful connections to each other.

Research on book clubs has demonstrated a variety of positive impacts on adolescents. George (2001) found that YAL book clubs helped urban middle school students become more engaged, participate more actively, and gain a deeper appreciation for literature. Gibbons, Dail, and Stallworth (2006) found that group reading promoted student engagement and enhanced social interactions. Similarly, Daniels (2002) found that book clubs improved achievement scores, increased enjoyment of and engagement in reading, promoted multicultural awareness, and provided social outlets for students.

Furthermore, Daniels (2002) cited research that demonstrates benefits to a variety of populations including urban students, incarcerated adolescents, resistant learners, homeless children, children living in poverty, and second language learners. Other researchers found that book clubs helped prepare youth to live in diverse societies (Raphael, Florio-Ruane, and George, 2001), assisted adolescent females in their sense of agency (Smith, 2000), and enhanced Latinos' understanding of themselves (Broughton, 2002).

Vyas (2004) also found benefits in book clubs, specifically with Asian students who experienced a sense of identity duality. By using texts that illuminate the experiences of people of color, book clubs have also enabled young women to find their voice and increase their self-esteem (Boston and Baxley, 2007), while also providing a safe space to grapple with topics such as discrimination (Brooks, Browne, and Hampton, 2008).

CONTEXT

This one-year study was conducted in an urban high school in the Northeast with a population of four hundred students who are primarily Latinos (55 percent) and African Americans (35 percent), 68 percent of whom qualify for free or reduced lunch. My own position within the context is unique in that I am an instructional coach and literacy intervention teacher at the school. I never, however, taught the participants in this study. This chapter includes data from two book clubs, all consisting of adolescent females of color. The younger book club consisted of four ninth grade and one tenth grade girl, of whom two were African American and three Latina. The older book club consisted of seven eleventh grade girls, of whom two were African American and five Latina.

In terms of book selection, the participants came to the group with their own suggestions or we visited the library together. For the entire year, the young women voted on the texts—all of which were YAL with female protagonists. Book clubs met once a week, during lunch or after school. Sessions lasted approximately forty-five minutes and followed a "loose" agenda: five to ten minutes of check-in about significant issues (not limited to book conversations), thirty to thirty-five minutes of discussion or reading aloud of the text, and five to ten minutes of debriefing conversations, book club processes, and reading plans for the following week.

As a facilitator, my most important task was to provide a safe atmosphere with a consistent structure. This safe space required me to listen.

Simultaneously, I ensured that all voices were heard, a difficult feat especially when the participants were enthusiastic. Sometimes I interrupted them when they talked over one another or when someone's voice was not heard. Sometimes I elicited responses from quieter group members. And, sometimes, if the group got too far away from the book, I brought them back to home base: the text.

In terms of questioning, the participants led discussions and came prepared with questions on Post-it notes. I asked questions frequently as well. It was useful when I had notes in advance to direct the groups, because the participants stayed much more focused. However, when I did this, I worried it took away from the student-centered nature of the book club. Additionally, I felt that when doing so, I was leading their interpretations. Therefore, this more directive structure only lasted for the first month as a way to scaffold the book club process and to model asking rich questions. The rest of the year I asked much more general questions so as to push their thinking about the texts and keep them on-task, including the following: What did you think about the book? How did it relate to your own experiences, identities, and/or communities? Can you say more on that? Why do you think the author made that decision?

METHODS

Qualitative data were collected from many sources, including observations, interviews, and book club discussion transcripts. Pre-interviews were conducted with all twelve females to document familial, school, and literacy background information, and post-interviews were used to capture their reflections of the book club. All interviews were recorded and transcribed. Book club discussions were also recorded and transcribed for a total of twenty-two book club meetings with the younger group and twenty-four meetings with the older group. A field log was also kept to record notes of the context, analyses, and reflections.

Data were analyzed during and after data collection. Once transcriptions were done, using qualitative methods (Bogdan and Biklen, 2003), I read through the transcripts several times. On the first read, I began with a holistic lens to target categories so as to develop a coding system. Codes were initially made for larger "content" concepts including issues such as identity, schooling, and relationships. I then read through the transcripts a second time, coding for evidence of the students' use of Common Core Standards. Textbox 7.1 outlines the standards that participants demonstrated throughout the year:

TEXTBOX 7.1: CCSS USED BY STUDENTS

CCSS.ELA-LITERACY.CCRA.R.1: Read to determine what the text says explicitly and to make inferences (coded as R1a); cite evidence to support conclusions (coded as R1b).
CCSS.ELA-LITERACY.CCRA.R.2: Determine central ideas or themes and analyze their development (coded as R2a); summarize key details (coded as R2b).
CCSS.ELA-LITERACY.CCRA.R.3: Analyze how and why individuals, events, or ideas develop and interact (coded as R3).
CCSS.ELA-LITERACY.CCRA.R.6: Assess how point of view or purpose shapes the content and style (coded as R6).

Since so many of the responses were connective ones—both to the literature and to each other—another code was added, "Connections," which included personal and intertextual connections. Other categories that emerged were "Clarifications"—which occurred when participants asked each other questions about the text—and "Off-Text," which occurred when they had conversations that were not directly related to the books. I then read through the transcripts a third time, checking my codes and revising initial categories if needed.

SUMMARIZING AS A WAY OF ENTERING THE STORY (CCRA.R.2)

Summarizing the text is a foundational aspect of the conversations during the book club meetings, as these were used as gateways that allowed for deeper interpretations. For the participants, summaries represented multiple purposes. Sometimes they had not done the reading. In most of these cases, they waited until the next week for others to catch up but sometimes those who had not read wanted to be filled in—either to make the decision to keep reading or because they did not want to read the book anymore but still wanted to know the ending.

Other times, the adolescents used these summaries as springboards into more in-depth analyses. An example of this occurred while the older group discussed *The True Meaning of Cleavage* (Fredericks, 2004), where the purpose of the summary was to inform Carla, a new member, about the text:

Yoana: It's about these two best friends named Sari and Jess and they're just starting high school. This girl Sari—she likes this senior named David Cole.

Keisha: David Cole who is going out with Thea.

Gina: Can I continue from there? So then Sari, she got a crush on this guy, right? She saw him at the Halloween party . . . that the whole school is going to go to and Jess who is more down-to-earth she was like no. They have this thing they do every Halloween, and Sari didn't want to. They were split, and at the party, Sari saw a guy and she starts talking to him.

Keisha: So then Jess and this boy Danny hang out one day. They went out and then he went to her house and he gave her that picture.

Gina: So they have these things in common but he's super geekish and she's like I don't even want to be associated with you. I don't want to be seen with you, but he always follows her because he thinks they're friends.

This summary sounded much like a choir with the group members continually adding to the plot, filling in missing details that the current speaker may have missed. While students summarized, they continually cited textual evidence (CCRA.R.1) as a way to flesh out their collective summary.

Another example of summarizing was with *Party Girl* (Ewing, 1999). Here the purpose of the summary was to explain the book to Gina, who decided she did not like the text but still wanted to know the ending. Keisha explained, "Kata and Ana are best friends. In the beginning they go to a party. They dance and then they walk around. They walk home because they didn't get on the bus. Skip to the good part. She dies and a car pulls up. She's standing there. A guy points a gun at her and Kata ducks behind another car." In this explanation, Keisha filtered her summary to relevant textual details (CCRA.R.1). She did not provide minutia, but distinguished between what Gina needed to know and what she did not need to know.

The younger group participated in this same process. Like Carla, Sofia also joined the group later in the year. When she entered the book club, the group had just finished reading *The Earth, My Butt and Other Round Things* (Mackler, 2003). Tia summarized the book for Sofia:

It's about this girl named Virginia Shreves and she's messing with this guy named Froggy. . . . She's like pretty rich. She lives in a penthouse apartment. Her mom is a teen psychologist and her dad is—what is her dad? I don't know what her dad does. Her brother was a college student. Her sister works at Peace Corps in Africa. So you know, her life is pretty normal. She doesn't talk to Froggy in school but her mom is harassing her about losing weight and in the middle of the book her brother comes home from college because the dean calls and says he date-raped this girl. . . . So he has to stay home from school for a while or until the situation is figured out. What makes it so funny is . . . their mom is treating him like "Oh, you want some cupcakes?" And yet Virginia's sitting there like can I spend Thanksgiving in Walla Walla with my friend Shannon

and her mom goes "No, we're spending Thanksgiving here." All the time telling
her brother, "Oh, you wanna go outside, go outside." Like, what sense does that
make? That sounds like my parents. They're so sexist.

This last comment then sent the participants on a conversation about parents and how they treat boys and girls differently. Although originally the
purpose of this summary was to inspire Sofia to read the text, it then became
a springboard into a larger societal issue around gender inequity.

As seen above, depending on the purpose and on the level of interest and
engagement with the books, these summaries were sometimes short and
simple, yet other times verbose and tangential. Sometimes they sounded like
a chorus with group members continually adding to the story. However, when
the plots were articulated, they were useful to participants who had missed
the reading. Furthermore, they were needed to clarify the plot and characters
so that they could move on to more inferential and higher-level conversations
required by the Common Core.

CLARIFYING AND REVISING INTERPRETATIONS (CCRA.R.1)

Another reading strategy (not required by Common Core—but critical in
helping students read metacognitively) was that of textual clarifications.
During this process, students acknowledged a lack of clarity and sought
out information in order to construct meaning. Often the group did this by
rereading sections of the text to find the answers to their questions. This kind
of close reading is exactly the shift that Common Core wants our students
to make when reading texts. An example occurred with the younger group
while they read *The True Meaning of Cleavage*. Sofia was confused about
what happened at the party:

Sofia: The New Year's Eve party—what happens?

Tia: David will only see Sari every two weeks so he won't get caught by his
girlfriend. Here I'll show you. [*Tia finds the passage and reads it aloud.*]

Betsy: He did her and then just like—

Tia: Dropped her.

Sofia: He didn't do her.

Tia: She did something. [*The participants laugh.*] And then after she did something and then he dropped her like it's hot.

From here, the group members then made personal connections of what they would have done if they were in this same situation. Although this conversation certainly addressed racy material (oral sex), many of them would not have gotten the underlying nuances of what the author was implying, thus demonstrating the Standard of inferences (CCRA.R.1). It is through this kind of discussion that the participants understood what occurred in the book so they could then discuss the implications of such behaviors. The process of thinking aloud allowed the readers to clarify issues that they could not in isolation.

Sometimes the clarifications, however, were not so inferential. Sometimes they were more about understanding specific pieces of a text. For example, while reading *Tiger Eyes* (Blume, 1982) aloud, Tia called "candy stripers," "candy strippers." Once I explained what a candy striper was, they all laughed. Tia said, "I was wondering why she would put 'stripper' on her college application!"

Again, meaning is constructed through our shared reading and interpretation of the text. Other clarifications were to discuss and negotiate inferences the participants made during their individual reading. Collectively, they worked to understand the text at much deeper levels. For example, while reading *Forever* (Blume, 1996), the younger group tried to establish the relationship between two of the minor characters, Erica and Arty:

Betsy: Wait, but I didn't get it. Did Erica like Arty?

Sofia: I think she liked Arty but not in that way. I think she wanted to help him more.

Tia: I feel bad for Arty. He tried to kill himself.

Betsy: He did with the shower curtain.

Tia: I don't know. He was confusing throughout the whole book.

Betsy: He was all happy in the play and then all of a sudden he started hanging out with Erica.

Fay: She probably confused him, because she probably tried to force him . . . into liking girls more than boys.

Tia: So why did he tell her "I don't know, maybe"?

Sofia: Maybe he didn't want to admit that he had a lot of psychological problems. . . . I think Erica added to the issues, 'cause although she tried to help him, he was like if he knew he was gay and then she was trying to help him he probably felt worse.

During this clarification process, the participants demonstrate their skill in Common Core Standard 1—using textual evidence to strengthen textual interpretations and inferences.

These same kinds of clarifications arose with the older group as well. While reading *Sisterhood of the Traveling Pants* (Brahares, 2003), Gina asked what happened on the beach with Bridgette and the coach because she did not understand:

Julie: They had sex! Look. [*Julie reads aloud from the text.*]

Gina: I was so lost from that part to when she was talking about her mother. . . . I didn't understand why she got sad for her mother when that happened but now I understand that she needs her mother to give her advice. Thank you, guys! This is why I love book club!

Making clarifications and discussing inferences allowed for a deeper construction of meaning.

This revision of understanding is evidence of growth that should be encouraged so that our students feel safe taking risks and begin to ask critical questions to aid in their comprehension and interpretations. Many of the book club members struggled with reading, and these discussions enhanced their understanding. For Gina, she read too fast, so these discussions forced her to slow down and construct deeper meaning. For students such as Yoana or Betsy, whose reading comprehension is below grade level, these conversations deepened their understanding.

EVALUATING AND ASSESSING THE TEXT (CCRA.R.6)

A frequent conversation for the groups was evaluating the text, Standard 6. Here, students consider not only the author's agenda, but also the author's effectiveness as a writer. These conversations were useful in the beginning of the meetings to inspire conversation. For example, while discussing *The True Meaning of Cleavage,* the younger group immediately shared that they loved the book. I pushed these initial assessments by asking them what about the book made it good reading. Joy explained, "How she writes. She's telling you—I don't know, she just makes the characters do some crazy things. Like one day they're all nice and then they're friendly and then they're like don't talk to me. I don't want to talk to you."

Here, Joy articulates the aspects of the author's writing that makes the storyline interesting. Joy's evaluation then led to a conversation about the relationship between Sari and Jess and our session lunged to a start. The same was true for the older group as they read the same text. Pat began the session by stating, "I liked Jess's character," which then led to a conversation about the complexities of Jess's situation.

Additionally, toward the end of this book club meeting (as was true for most sessions), the group members returned to a "wrap-up" or assessment of the text as a whole. When leaving a book, I always asked for their final reflections of the text and author:

> **Gina:** It didn't work for me 'cause I was going through the same thing and it was like why would she do that? I don't understand why Sari was acting like that. . . . They never explained in the book—like why would she treat her like this. . . . I just didn't understand it and that got me upset.

> **Pat:** I think the book worked for me because in the end, even though Jess did a bad thing and told everybody what she was doing, she was always there till the end. Even when [Sari did those things], she was always there.

> **Yoana:** It was alright. It's just the ending. . . . I thought that David was going to end up with Sari and then the whole drama for nothing whatever just got on my nerves.

The participants continued this conversation, weaving in and out from evaluating the text to analyzing characters, all the time citing textual evidence as a way to back up their assessments (CCRA.R.1). Similar to summarizing, evaluating the text was an entry point to more inferential conversations where they worked to co-construct meanings.

ANALYZING AND MAKING CONNECTIONS (CCRA.R.3)

One of the richest conversations about books was discussion of the characters and how the participants made connections with them. Participants discussed the characters as if they were real, analyzing their behaviors and decisions, and connecting these to their own lives. Often the girls started with personal connections, which led them to deeper character analysis, where they dissected and unraveled the protagonists' actions. An example of this occurred while the older group read *The True Meaning of Cleavage*:

> **Julie:** I love Jess. She's so down-to-earth.

> **Keisha:** I'm mad though that she didn't open her mouth about stuff that Sari was doing to her. Like open your mouth!

> **Julie:** Sari is so stupid. . . . At one point it got on my nerves because after all that, after you losing your friend—well, you didn't really lose her—but you

know what I mean, putting him ahead. He wasn't even worth all that. You don't even know him like that. He's just using you.

The younger group also analyzed the relationship between the two characters, Jess and Sari.

Joy: Sari—they describe her as pretty and everything and she's always into that stuff and fixing herself but Jess doesn't really care. She likes to draw.

Sofia: I agree with what Joy said because Sari is more open about high school. She's like, "Okay, it's time to have fun." High school is time to have fun, get a boyfriend, look hot, whatever . . . but Jess is more like it's just high school.

Tia: [Sari's] focusing on the wrong things.

Betsy: She's the kind of girl where—when you're entering high school, it doesn't mean all books and education. She wants to do what teenagers do. Teenagers, they go out, this that and the third, but I think she's going to get herself caught up in too many things.

Here, both book groups cited textual evidence (CCRA.R.1) from the texts in order to create a deeper understanding and interpretation of the characters and their motivations.

Within the analysis of the characters, the two groups continually made judgments about the characters' behaviors—often stating what they would have done instead. This identification and association happened repeatedly and was an important part of their aesthetic response to the reading and connection with each other. For example, while reading *Speak* (Anderson, 1999), the younger group was furious with the main character's friends:

Tia: I was mad at Heather.

Tia: I'm like first off if you don't want to be friends with her, then don't be friends with her. Why you going to come back to her and ask her for a favor? She don't want to talk to you, so then why are you bothering her with this favor?

Fay: She only comes to her if she needs something—like help with the Marthas.

Betsy: They were in the lunchroom or something and and she was like "This is very hard for me to say but we can't be friends anymore."

Tia: I would have slapped her.

Betsy: Why would you go through all that just to be my friend and then all of a sudden stop. . . . She was like "I think you need help." No, I think you do.

Here the participants are deeply immersed and engaged with the reading, participating in critical perspective-taking, where they imagined what they would have done if they were in a similar situation. Notice that Betsy shifts her pronouns to first person: It is not "her" friend but "my" friend. Tia has the same vicarious experience, stating, "You don't talk to me," as if she is living through the experience of the characters. This social-cognitive process required them to not only recall their individual reading experiences but to relate their experiences to the characters and to each other, thus considering alternate interpretations.

The older group also got upset with the characters and discussed what they would have done in similar situations, as evidenced below with Upstate (Buckhanon, 2006), when the group members criticize Natasha's stepfather:

> **Keisha:** Come on, people! If you are with my mother and you're a grown-ass man and you want to smoke weed in my house. That's up to you if you want to smoke weed or not in the house. Alright, go ahead. Do it then. But if I don't have any money and you say go to the store for me, you better be handing over some cash 'cause I'm not spending no money on you.

> **Gina:** He has the munchies and he tells her to go to the store!

> **Keisha:** Get your own damn snow cone! You got money enough to buy weed and smoke and blunts. Ya'll need to get your own snacks. I'm not buying your snacks.

Immediately, like Betsy, Keisha shifts perspectives, placing herself in the main characters' shoes. These scripts demonstrate the participants' analysis and connection with the characters. Their arguments lead to a deeper understanding of not just the text and its major themes, but to larger societal and community issues, and they do so by transporting themselves into the texts and living vicariously through the characters. The participants situated themselves within the texts and discussed what they would do if they were in the same kinds of situations, thus allowing for a deeper and more intense interpretation of the characters.

IMPLICATIONS FOR ENGLISH LANGUAGE ARTS

In terms of the implications, I will begin with Julie, who exclaimed at the end of one meeting: "You know what would be mad hot? If we could do this in English!" Julie's comment reveals the many ways we can use these findings when reenvisioning our ELA classrooms. The most obvious way is to implement more book clubs within schools, following the model I have outlined here as a way to provide supplemental support for our adolescents. We also need to think about how to differentiate our instruction more effectively by integrating book clubs into our classrooms.

This research study adds to Daniels's (2002) work, demonstrating that student-led literature groups increase student enjoyment of and engagement in reading, expand students' discourse opportunities, enhance perspectives on social issues, and provide social outlets for students. Book clubs also help us to differentiate instruction. While the Common Core has increased the levels at which students must be reading, it does not mean that we get students in our classroom who are at these levels.

Creating these high Lexile text measures does not mean our students will miraculously "get there" just by providing them with tougher texts. In fact, if we do this, our students will shut down. Moss (2013) explains that classroom texts should pose challenges that invite students to grow, however, not at the expense of losing our students' sense of engagement, self-confidence, and motivation.

A golden opportunity can be created in using book clubs and YAL in that we can provide the scaffolding and differentiation needed in order to help our students grow as readers (Groenke and Scherff, 2010). For whole-class texts, we can read challenging, higher-level literature (classics or YAL) aloud and practice the Common Core. Students can then use young adult literature in order to practice in small groups the skills with texts that are at their level—and that they are interested in.

Providing students with books at their level means providing our readers with successful reading experiences where they do not experience frustration. Matching students' Lexile level to appropriate texts allows them to be sufficiently challenged in order to grow as independent readers. This kind of gradual scaffolded release of responsibility for reading instruction has been demonstrated as effective through multiple research studies for improving our students' literacy levels (Allington, 2012; Fisher and Frey, 2007).

Furthermore, Thompson (2014) urges ELA teachers to take part in professional conversations, where we begin to be more thoughtful about the content we are teaching—and why. We need to advocate for ourselves and for what we know is best for our students, especially as more curricula are being developed and mandated at the state level that *only* is grounded in the CCSS exemplar texts that are clearly not representative or appropriate for all of our students.

We should also keep in mind that CCSS tells us that we need to think *beyond* the Lexile levels of texts, looking equally at the readers in our classrooms, the tasks being required of them, and the qualitative textual measurements, such as its meaning, language, structure, and knowledge demands (NGA, 2010). Because qualitative measures hold equal weight, Beach,

---

TEXTBOX 7.2: CULTURALLY RELEVANT YAL

- **American Indians in Children's Literature:** americanindiansinchildrensliterature.blogspot.com
- **The Brown Bookshelf:** thebrownbookshelf.com
- **CBC Diversity Committee of the Children's Book Council:** www.cbcdiversity.com
- **De Colores:** The Raza Experience in Books for Children: decoloresreviews.blogspot.com
- **Disability in Kidlit:** disabilityinkidlit.wordpress.com
- **Diversity in YA:** www.diversityinya.com
- **GayYA:** LGBTQIA + Characters in YA Fiction and LGBTQIA + YA Authors: www.gayya.org
- **Latin@s in Kid Lit:** latinosinkidlit.com
- **Malindo Lo:** www.malindalo.com
- **Reading in Color:** blackteensread2.blogspot.com
- **Rich in Color:** richincolor.com

Haertling Thein, and Webb (2012) ask us to move beyond the exemplar list so that our texts are reflective of our students' interests, identities, communities, and cultural backgrounds.

In selecting diverse texts, however, we need to also be careful in selecting books that are realistic, yet do not perpetuate stereotypes. Currently, there is a disconcerting lack of representation in YAL. Textbox 7.2 provides resources for locating more culturally relevant and responsive YAL.

In addition to rethinking of texts, ELA teachers might also choose to go beyond the Common Core skills, especially for our reluctant or struggling readers. Critical strategies such as asking questions and making connections are essential as students begin to engage with more challenging and complex texts. In allowing our students to ask questions and make personal connections, they may be able to better interpret and analyze what they are reading, as demonstrated by the conversations in this study.

Daniels (2002) supports these kinds of student-centered and student-driven transactions, stating, "The pathways to analysis, to more sophisticated and defensible interpretations of literature, must go through personal response, not around it" (p. 38). This position is situated within other theorists (Rosenblatt, 1995; Twomey, 2007), who all advocated for an experiential-based classroom that is grounded in reader response theory and the transactional nature of reading.

Overall, in reflecting on YAL-centered book clubs—whether outside or inside the classroom—we must provide students with alternative and innovative support systems, and at the same time, begin to approach education in a more differentiated and culturally responsive way, where all students receive assistance in their literacy development so that we can create a society of engaged readers who continue to enjoy, reflect on, and connect to literature long after they have left our classrooms.

REFERENCES

Allington, R. L. (2012). *What really matters for struggling readers: Designing research-based programs* (3rd ed.). Boston, MA: Allyn & Bacon.

Anderson, L. H. (1999). *Speak.* New York, NY: Farrar, Straus, Giroux.

Beach, R., Haertling Thein, A., and Webb, A. (2012). *Teaching to exceed the English language arts Common Core State Standards.* New York, NY: Routledge.

Blume, J. (1982). *Tiger eyes.* New York, NY: Laurel-Leaf.

Blume, J. (1996). *Forever.* New York, NY: Pocket.

Bogdan, R. C., and Biklen, S. K. (2003). *Qualitative research for education: An introduction to theory and methods* (4th ed.). New York, NY: Pearson.

Booth, C. (2006). *Tyrell.* New York, NY: Push/Scholastic.

Boston, G. H., and Baxley, T. (2007). Living the literature: Race, gender construction, and black female adolescents. *Urban Education, 42*(5), 560–81.

Brahares, A. (2003). *Sisterhood of the traveling pants.* New York, NY: Delacorte.

Brooks, W., Browne, S., and Hampton, G. (2008). "There ain't no accounting for what folks see in their own mirrors": Considering colorism within a Sharon Flake narrative. *Journal of Adolescent and Adult Literacy, 51*(8), 660–69.

Broughton, M. A. (2002). The performance and construction of subjectivities of early adolescent girls in book club discussion groups. *Journal of Literacy Research, 34*(1), 1–38.

Buckhanon, K. (2006). *Upstate.* New York, NY: St. Martin's.

Coats, K. (2011). Young adult literature: Growing up, in theory. In S. A. Wolf, K. Coats, P. Enciso, and C. A. Jenkins (eds.), *Handbook of research on children's and young adult literature* (pp. 315–29). New York, NY: Routledge.

Curtis, C. P. (2000). *The Watsons go to Birmingham—1963.* New York: Laurel-Leaf.

Daniels, H. (2002). *Literature circles* (2nd ed.). Portland, ME: Stenhouse.

Ericson, B. O. (ed.) (2001). *Teaching reading in high school English classes.* Urbana, IL: NCTE.

Ewing, L. (1999). *Party girl.* New York, NY: Knopf.

Fisher, D., and Frey, N. (2007). Implementing a schoolwide literacy framework: Improving achievement in an urban elementary school. *The Reading Teacher, 61*(1), 32–45.

Fredericks, M. (2004). *The true meaning of cleavage.* New York, NY: SimonPulse.

George, M. A. (2001). What's the big idea? Integrating young adult literature in the middle school. *English Journal, 90*(3), 74–81.

Gibbons, L. C., Dail, J. S., and Stallworth, B. J. (2006). Young adult literature in the English curriculum today: Classroom teachers speak out. *The ALAN Review, 33*(3), 53–61.

Glaus, M. (2013). Text complexity and young adult literature: Establishing its place. *Journal of Adolescent and Adult Literacy, 57*(5), 407–16.

Groenke, S. L., and Scherff, L. (2010). *Teaching YA lit through differentiated instruction.* Urbana, IL: NCTE.

Haddon, M. (2003). *Curious incident of the dog in the night-time.* New York, NY: Vintage.

Henk, W., Marinack, B., and Melnick, S. (2013). Measuring the reader self-perception of adolescents. *Journal of Adolescent and Adult Literacy, 56*(4), 311–20.

Mackler, C. (2003). *The earth, my butt, and other round things.* New York, NY: Candlewick.

Moss, B. (2013). Making the common core text exemplars accessible to middle graders. *Voices from the Middle, 20*(4), 43–46.

Myers, W. D. (1999). *Monster.* New York, NY: Amistad.

National Governors Association (NGA) Center for Best Practices and Council of Chief State School Officers. (2010). *Common core state standards for English language arts and literacy in history/social studies, science and technical subjects.* Washington, DC: Authors.

Ostenson, J., and Wadham, R. (2012). Young adult literature and the common core: A surprisingly good fit. *American Secondary Education, 41*(1), 4–13.

Raphael, T. E., Florio-Ruane, S., and George, M. (2001). Book club plus: A conceptual framework to organize literacy instruction. *Language Arts, 79*(2), 159–66.

Rapp, A. (2009). *Punkzilla.* New York, NY: Candlewick.

Rosenblatt, L. M. (1995). *Literature as exploration* (5th ed.). New York, NY: MLA.

Santoli, S. P., and Wagner, M. E. (2004). Promoting young adult literature: The other "real" literature. *American Secondary Education, 33*(1), 65–75.

Smith, S. (2000). Talking about "real stuff": Explorations of agency and romance in an all-girls' book club. *Language Arts, 78*(1), 30–38.

Stallworth, B. J. (2006). The relevance of young adult literature. *Educational Leadership, 63*(7), 59–63.

Thompson, K. H. (2014). Beyond the stacks: Why high school English teachers should be talking about books. *English Journal, 103*(6), 38–44.

Twomey, S. (2007). Reading "woman": Book club pedagogies and the literary imagination. *Journal of Adolescent and Adult Literacy, 50*(5), 398–407.

Vyas, S. (2004). Exploring bicultural identities of Asian students through the analytic window of a literature club. *Journal of Adolescent and Adult Literacy, 48*(1), 12–23.

Chapter Eight

Annotated Resources for the Classroom Teacher

Judith A. Hayn, Kent Layton, and Heather A. Olvey

The idea of teaching literature across the content areas is daunting to many teachers, particularly in the math and science disciplines. Many wonder why all teachers have to now be accountable for what has always been the responsibility of English language arts (ELA) teachers. The reality of our present-day work world, coupled with the Common Core State Standards (CCSS) that must be implemented, forces today's educators to chart new territories and use new resources. Young adult literature can be used effectively in all classes, whether it is by using an entire book to teach a certain topic, or by pulling out part of the assigned novel to create Problem-Based-Learning units, or simply problem posing.

Steven Bickmore and Leylja Emiraliyeva-Pitre (2011/2012) argue (in their article "Teaching Diverse Young Adult Literature in Harmony with the Common Core State Standards: Is It Still Just About the Characters, the Plot, the Setting?") that as a result of studying several young adult novels in a graduate-level course, the students all agreed that the YAL books they read can, in fact, be taught in conjunction with the standards.

While conversation about a novel naturally begins with the reader's connection to a character or plot, that is perfectly acceptable even outside an ELA class because that is how the reader begins to analyze what is happening. We have to understand the what, where, and when before we can dig deeper. Bickmore and Emiraliyeva-Pitre also point out that "even when these graduate students disliked a novel, they did not dismiss the teachable moment" (p. 22). To help you find your teachable moment, in whatever discipline you teach, here is a list of teacher resources and suggested contemporary YA texts sorted by content area.

TEACHER REFERENCES

Articles

Alsup, J. (2013). Teaching literature in an age of text complexity. *Journal of Adolescent & Adult Literacy, 57*(3), 181–84.

> In her commentary, Alsup argues that fiction does meet stated criteria for complex texts.

Bickmore, S. T., and Pitre, L. (2014). Moving from a novice to an expert reader/ teacher of young adult literature. *The Florida English Journal, 50*(1), 37–47.

> Bickmore and Pitre outline the steps to take to become an expert in YAL.

Conners, S. P., and Shepard, I. (2011/2012). Reframing arguments for teaching YA literature in an age of common core. *SIGNAL Journal, 35*(3), 6–10.

> This article presents teachers with a well-documented argument favoring the use of YA literature to meet the Common Core State Standards.

Dyer, S. (2014). Read this, not that: Why and how I'll use young adult literature in my classroom. *Virginia English Journal, 64*(1), 33–43.

> Virginia Monseau's observations in an English teacher's classroom address the inclusion of multiculturalism through YAL.

Elish-Piper, L., Wold, L. S., and Schwingendorf, K. Scaffolding high school students' reading of complex tests using linked sets. *Journal of Adolescent & Adult Literacy, 57*(7), 565–74.

> The authors posit linked text sets as an approach to unite teens with complex texts required in CCSS. The article shows the strategies in action in a tenth grade ELA class.

Fang, Z. (2013). Disciplinary literacy in science. *Journal of Adolescent & Adult Literacy, 57*(4), 274–78.

> The author argues for the use of trade books in teaching science.

Glaus, M. (2014). Text complexity and young adult literature. *Journal of Adolescent & Adult Literacy, 57*(5), 407–16.

> The authors make the case for using YAL to teach CCSS and examine qualitative evaluations of three works defined as textually complex and yet engaging for teens.

Roberts, M. (2012). Teaching young adult literature. *The English Journal, 102*(1), 92–95.

> This article outlines steps for ELA teachers to follow to guide other content area teachers in how to teach YAL in their classes. It includes suggestions of YAL to use in non-ELA classes.

Books

Bushman, J. H., and Hans, K. P. (2005). Young adult literature and the classics. In J.
    H. Bushman (ed.), *Using young adult literature in the English classroom* (4th ed.),
    (pp. 167–85). Upper Saddle River, NJ: Pearson Education.
    This chapter explores the relationship between young adults and the literature
    they read and alternatives to using a curriculum based primarily on the classics.
Cole, P. B. (2009). *Young adult literature in the 21st century.* New York, NY:
    McGraw Hill.
    A great resource that discusses many of the genres within YAL, gives lists of
    possible titles within each genre, has YAL author comment boxes, and gives
    many examples of literacy strategies to teach YAL.
Hayn, J. A., and Kaplan, J. S. (2012). *Teaching young adult literature today: Insights,
    considerations and perspectives for the classroom teacher.* Plymouth, MA: Row-
    man & Littlefield.
    Experts in the field tackle important topics in YAL.
Knickerbocker, J. L., Brueggeman, M. A., and Rycik, J. A. (2012). *Literature for
    young adults: Books and more for contemporary readers.* Scottsdale, AZ: Hol-
    comb Hathaway.
    This text includes chapters on film, graphic novels, picture books, and illustrated
    literature, along with literary nonfiction.
Wadham, R. L., and Ostenson, J. W. (2013). *Integrating young adult literature
    through the Common Core Standards.* Santa Barbara, CA: Libraries Unlimited.
    This book offers teachers an introduction to YAL, an in-depth discussion of
    how YAL can work with the CCSS, and how teachers can evaluate a book's text
    complexity. It also discusses inquiry learning and walks one through the process
    of creating a unit plan by using an essential question or theme.

Websites

www.adlit.org.
    A website full of articles and suggestions of how to teach YAL.
ncte.org.
    The National Council of Teachers of English's website offers many articles on
    how to teach YAL, as well as offering backing for the validity of the genre by
    giving teachers support on how to deal with censorship issues.

ADDITIONAL YA FICTION SELECTIONS
BY CONTENT DISCIPLINE

Arts

Barnaby, H. (2012). *Wonder show*. New York, NY: Houghton Mifflin Harcourt Children's Books.

> Portia just wants to belong, and perhaps a traveling freak show is the place.

Calame, D. (2012). *Call the shots*. Somerville, MA: Candlewick.

> Three guys have pulled off schemes before, but now they try to make a low-budget horror film.

Federle, T. (2013). *Better Nate than ever*. New York, NY: Simon & Schuster Books for Young Readers.

> Nate goes to Broadway for a chance at musical stardom.

Waller, S. B. (2014). *A mad, wicked folly*. New York, NY: Viking Books for Young Readers.

> Victoria, at seventeen and living in 1909 London, pursues her dream of being an artist.

Zarr, S. (2013). *The Lucy variations*. New York, NY: Little Brown Books for Young Readers.

> Lucy plays piano to make others happy, so when she walks away, a young piano teacher shows her another way.

English

Harrington, L. (2012). *Alice Bliss*. New York, NY: Penguin Books.

> The story of a teenage girl whose father is sent to Afghanistan. Alice and her family deal with the separation from their father while he is away. This is a good book to use with students from military families.

Howe, K. (2014). *Conversion*. New York, NY: G.P. Putnam's Sons Books for Young Readers.

> Based on true events from happenings in both 2011 and the Salem Witch Trials, this story alternates between the two time periods telling a similar story of teen's seemingly supernatural behavior. The content and issues in this text also would match well with students reading *The Crucible*.

Levithan, D. (2013). *Two boys kissing*. New York, NY: Random House Books for Young Readers.

> Harry and Craig vie for the Guinness World Record for the longest kiss.

Lockhart, E. (2014). *We were liars*. New York, NY: Delacorte Press.

> Cadence is a member of the Sinclair family, a wealthy family who spends every summer on their private island. One particular summer Cadence can't remember what happened, but she knows it was traumatic. This text would be great to use when teaching about unreliable narrators.

Newman, L. (2012). *October mourning: A song for Matthew Shepard.* Somerville, MA: Candlewick.
>   This moving book reveals the 1998 murder of Matthew Shepard through a hate crime. Using poetry and various points of view, the author reveals the horror of this news-making event.

Reedy, T. (2014). *If you're reading this.* New York, NY: Arthur A. Levine Books.
>   The story of a teenage boy whose father was killed in Afghanistan when he was younger. Mike comes of age in his father's absence. This text also is a great book to read to help students understand and explore the sacrifices military families make for their country.

Rowell, R. (2013). *Eleanor & Park.* New York, NY: Macmillan/St. Martin's Griffin.
>   An unlikely pair of outsiders find each other in modern-day New York City.

Schneider, R. (2014). *The beginning of everything.* New York, NY: Katherine Tegen Books.
>   Ezra Faulkner survives a terrible car wreck and has to come to terms with who he is now that he can no longer play tennis. In addition, he loses his girlfriend, and no longer feels like he fits in with his crowd of friends, all while falling in love with someone he never would have paid attention to before. This text would complement students' reading of *The Great Gatsby.*

Sullivan, T. (2013). *Golden boy.* New York, NY: G. P. Putnam's Sons.
>   This text tells the story of Habo, who was born an albino in Tanzania, and how he suffers prejudice for being different. This text would integrate well with a variety of topics in social studies.

Health

Anderson, L. H. (2014). *The impossible knife of memory.* New York, NY: Viking Books for Young Readers.
>   This story deals with themes of memory, PTSD, and a daughter becoming the responsible party in a story about a teenage girl with a father suffering from post-traumatic stress.

Cooner, D. (2013). *Skinny.* New York, NY: Scholastic/Point.
>   Ever hopes that weight-loss surgery will stop the voice in her head that whispers "Skinny"; however, losing weight does not cure her insecurities.

Green, J. (2012). *The fault in our stars.* New York, NY: Penguin/Dutton Juvenile.
>   This best-seller traces the story of two Cancer Kids, Hazel and Gus, who bond despite their different prognoses.

Howe, K. (2015). *Conversion.* New York, NY: Putnam.
>   Colleen seeks a solution to the mystery illness invading her school.

Metzger, L. (2013). *A trick of the light.* New York, NY: HarperCollins/Balzer & Bray.
>   Mike hears voices in his head. Is this normal, considering his anorexia and dysfunctional family?

Sedgwick, M. (2014). *She is not invisible.* New York, NY: Roaring Brook Press.
>   Blind teenager Laureth journeys to America to look for her writer father, who has vanished from his family in Britain.

Vaughn, L. R. (2013). *OCD, the dude, and me.* New York, NY: Penguin/Dial.

Danielle writes a "me-moir" of essays, journal entries, e-mails, and letters that detail her senior year as she struggles with OCD and life as a social outcast.

Vlahos, L. (2014). *The Scar Boys.* London, UK: Egmont.

A terrible childhood accident left Harry with physical and emotional scars that begin to heal with his band, The Scar Boys.

Mathematics

Bodeen, S. A. (2009). *The compound.* New York, NY: Square Fish.

Eli and his family have lived underground in a shelter for six years. Over time, Eli begins to wonder if their routine life is really as safe as they have assumed. This text provides ample opportunities to integrate math in the areas of measurements or rationing. (Roberts, 2012).

Green, J. (2008). *An abundance of Katherines.* New York, NY: Speak.

The story of an intellectual prodigy. Colin attempts to create a mathematical theorem that will predict how long romantic relationships can last. There are numerous references to math problems that could be explored in an effort to connect mathematical principles to everyday life.

Haddon, M. (2004). *The curious incident of the dog in the night time.* New York, NY: Knopf Doubleday/Vintage.

Christopher is fifteen and autistic. He does math problems in his head and eats only red food. The neighbor's poodle is killed, and he is falsely accused, so he uses deductive logic to try to solve the mystery.

Halpin, B. (2015). *Forever changes.* New York, NY: Open Road Media Teen & Tween.

Facing every day of her life with cystic fibrosis, Brianna is a brilliant math-minded teenager who has little to live for daily. In her final year of high school, she learns about a different kind of math that changes her perspective on life—forever.

Science

Barnes, J. L. (2013). *The naturals.* New York, NY: Hyperion/Miramax.

Cassie at seventeen is a natural profiler and joins a special FBI program where she is involved in mysterious activities.

Miller, L. (2014). *Free to fall.* New York, NY: HarperTeen.

Rory discovers a biotech conspiracy that could change civilization at her new prestigious prep school.

Schrefer, E. (2014). *Threatened.* New York, NY: Scholastic.

Luc is hired by a professor to help research chimpanzees, but when his mentor vanishes, Luc is left alone in the jungle.

Social Studies

Coats, J. A. (2012). *The wicked and the just*. New York, NY: Harcourt/Houghton Mifflin.

> Cecily, in the late thirteenth century, is a lady in occupied Wales. Her servant, Gwinny, refuses to bend to the upstart English tyrants.

Engle, M. (2013). *The lightning dream: Cuba's greatest abolitionist*. New York, NY: Houghton Mifflin Harcourt/HMH Books for Young Readers.

> A fictionalized account of the life of Cuban writer Gertrudis Gómez de Avellaneda leads to a discussion of Cuban freedom.

Follett, S. (2014). *The fog machine*. Chicago, IL: Lucky Sky Press.

> This historical fiction novel tells the story from the varying perspectives of three people growing up during the civil rights movement with references to historical events.

Gruener, R., Gruner, J., and Gratz, A. (2013). *Prisoner B-3087*. New York, NY: Scholastic.

> Yanek spends six years in ten concentration camps doing hard labor, but is determined to survive.

Wein, E. (2014). *Rose under fire*. New York, NY: Disney-Hyperion.

> This young adult historical novel is the story of an American pilot captured by the Nazis and sent to a concentration camp. Rose survives the horrible ordeals of the camp, eventually escapes, and later serves as a witness in trials against several Nazi war criminals.

Wiles, D. (2014). *Revolution*. New York, NY: Scholastic.

> The Freedom Summer of 1964 in Greenwood, Mississippi, is told by tween narrator Sunny. This is the second book in "The Sixties Trilogy." The first is *Countdown*, published in 2010.

REFERENCES

Bickmore, S. T., and Emiraliyeva-Pitre, L. (2012). Teaching diverse young adult literature in harmony with the Common Core State Standards: Is it still just about the characters, the plot, the setting? *SIGNAL Journal, 25*(3), 20–26.

Roberts, M. (2012). Teaching young adult literature. *The English Journal, 102*(1), 92–95.

Index

curriculum developers/teachers, 3, 4–5, 6
young adult fiction, 117–18
Etched in Clay (Cheng), 56
ethical dilemmas in science, 72
euthanasia, 71
evaluating and assessing text, 106–7
Evidence of Things Not Seen (Lane), 55–56
exemplar list, 3, 6, 97

fiction, YAL inclusion-themed examples, 87–88
figurative language, 43
First Part Last, The (Johnson)
  about, 20–21
  assessment, 24
  awards and honors, 18
  content area literacy and, 10–11
  four-corner debate, 23, 24
  jigsaw discussion, 23–24
  silent discussion, 23
  standards, 21
  survey, pre/post-reading, 21–23, 24
first-person point of view, 52
foreshadowing, 39, 47–48
Forever (Blume), 105–6
"40 Developmental Assets for Adolescents" survey, 27
four-corner debate, 23, 24
fulcrum texts, 70

general education. *See* inclusion students
Girl Who Saw Lions, The (Doherty), 56
graphic organizers, 62, 63–66
grief. *See Wintergirls* (Anderson)

health, in YAL, 118–19
health classes
  about, 16–17
  Common Core State Standards, 18
  First Part Last, The, 20–24
  National Health Education Standards, 18

resources, YAL titles with health themes, 18–19, 31–32
resources for implementation, 20
Staying Fat for Sarah Byrnes, 24–27
Wintergirls, 27–30
YAL as tool for literacy and content, 17–18, 31–32
YAL rationale and implementation, 18–20
historical/cultural knowledge, 38, 39–40

IDEA (Individuals with Disabilities Education Act), 78–80, 83
illusion/reality, 71–72
inclusion students. *See also* inclusion-themed young adult literature
  Common Core State Standards and, 82–84
  in general education classrooms, 79–80
  using YAL with, 89–91
inclusion-themed young adult literature. *See also* inclusion students
  examples of, 87–89
  fiction examples, 87–88
  nonfiction examples, 88–89
  purposes of, 86–87
  using, 89–90
Individuals with Disabilities Education Act (IDEA), 78–80, 83
informational texts, emphasis on, 97–98
Inside Out and Back Again (Lai), 12
instruction, anchoring, 70–72
interpretations, revising, 104–6
isolation/alienation, 71

jigsaw discussion, 23–24
journals, 8

knowledge, historical/cultural, 38, 39–40

Lexile text pairings, 99, 110
lifelong readers, 7, 86
limited omniscient point of view, 53
literacy, 10. *See also* content area literacy

About the Contributors

Patricia E. Bandré is the district reading instructional specialist for USD 305, Salina Public Schools in Salina, KS, where she has the opportunity to work with literacy coaches, teachers and students each day. Prior to this position, she taught in the intermediate grades for nine years and at the university level for ten years. Her research interests include the selection and use of read-alouds in the classroom and students' response to literature. Patricia currently serves as the president of the Children's Literature Assembly of the National Council of Teachers of English.

Karina R. Clemmons is an associate professor of secondary education at the University of Arkansas at Little Rock. Dr. Clemmons has taught English language arts and English for speakers of other languages classrooms in middle school, high school, and abroad. She researches, publishes, and presents in the areas of Young Adult Literature, teacher education, technology in education, and content literacy.

Sean P. Connors is an assistant professor of English education at the University of Arkansas. His scholarship and teaching focus on the application of diverse critical perspectives to young adult literature. Sean recently edited *The Politics of Panem: Challenging Genres*, a collection of critical essays about the Hunger Games series. He is the editor of *SIGNAL Journal*.

Christian Z. Goering is currently an associate professor of English education at the University of Arkansas where he directs the Northwest Arkansas Writing Project and the Center for Children & Youth. His scholarship focuses on understanding the uses of popular music in the teaching of English and on education policy. He recently served as coeditor of the *SIGNAL Journal* and a themed issue of *Reader*.

Nancy L. Hadaway has thirty-five years of experience in K–12 and university classrooms and is professor emerita, University of Texas at Arlington. She has been a member of several children's and young adult book award committees including the Orbis Pictus Committee, the Notable Books for a Global Society Committee, and the Outstanding International Book Committee and has coauthored or coedited several books about the use of children's and young adult literature with English learners.

Judith A. Hayn taught fifteen years in the public schools and is currently the interim associate dean in the College of Education and Health Professions at the University of Arkansas at Little Rock. Her research focuses on social justice issues in YAL; she has published numerous reviews, articles, and teacher curriculum materials. She coedited the 2012 text, *Teaching Young Adult Literature Today: Insights, Consideration, and Perspectives for the Classroom Teacher*, also published by Rowman & Littlefield.

Lisa A. Hazlett is professor of secondary education at The University of South Dakota. A regular presenter for NCTE and ALAN, she has published over thirty book chapters, brochures, and journal articles, all incorporating young adult literature. However, her preference and expertise is reviewing; she regularly reviews manuscripts, novels, and textbooks centering on young adult literature for numerous journals and publishing houses.

Crag Hill taught high school English for eighteen years in California and Idaho before embarking on a full-time position in English education. Currently an assistant professor of English education at University of Oklahoma, he edited *The Critical Merits of Young Adult Literature: Coming of Age,* published by Routledge in 2014. He is coeditor of a new journal, *Study and Scrutiny: Research on Young Adult Literature.*

Nikki Holland is currently a doctoral candidate in English at the University of Arkansas where she serves as director of the College Ready Writers' Program and as assistant director of the Northwest Arkansas Writing Project. Her doctoral research focuses on the interplay of argumentative writing and teacher development.

Jeffrey S. Kaplan, PhD, is an associate professor, School of Teaching, Learning, and Leadership, College of Education, University of Central Florida, Orlando. He is the former president of ALAN (2012–13), Assembly on Literature for Adolescents, and Research Connections editor for *The ALAN Review.* He is the current president of the National Council of Teachers of English Standing Committee Against Censorship (2015–17). He coedited with Judith Hayn, PhD, *Teaching Young Adult Literature Today: Insights, Considerations and Perspectives for the Classroom Teacher* (Rowman & Litttlefield, 2012). Educator and consultant, Jeffrey Kaplan is the author of many refereed publications on teaching strategies and methodologies for improving classroom instruction using literacy material geared for adolescent readers.

Kent Layton is currently an associate professor of reading education at the University of Arkansas at Little Rock where he teaches primarily in the graduate programs. He has authored book chapters and articles in the areas of text complexity issues, associated diagnostic assessments, technology and literacy, leadership of distance learning, content area reading, cloze procedure, and alternative certification pathways. In addition to his teaching, he has served as an education dean at the College of Coastal Georgia, the University of West Georgia, and Arkansas State University.

Amanda L. Nolen is the interim chair of the Psychology Department at the University of Arkansas at Little Rock. She was an associate professor of educational psychology prior to that position. She is the former chief operating officer for the Holmes Partnership, a national educational reform consortium. Nolen has published widely on topics such as emerging research methods, educational psychology, and teacher education reform.

Heather A. Olvey was a graduate research assistant for the Teacher Education Department of the University of Arkansas at Little Rock. She has presented her research in Young Adult Literature at the International Reading Association conference and has made contributions to several professional publications. She is currently teaching AP English in the Pulaski County AR School District.

Linda T. Parsons is an associate professor in the Department of Teaching and Learning on the Marion campus of The Ohio State University where she specializes in middle childhood literacy and young adult literature. Her research interests are inspired by her experience teaching in public schools before moving to the university and include the analysis of single titles and text sets of children's and young adult literature and readers' engagement with and response to literature. She has published numerous book chapters, articles, and book reviews.

Jody Polleck is an associate professor in adolescent literacy at Hunter College and a high school literacy intervention teacher and coach in New York City. Her research focus is on urban adolescents and culturally responsive and differentiated literacy instruction across the curriculum. Specifically, for the past decade, she has worked with urban adolescents in student-led book and writing clubs, exploring how these forums are effective in not only promoting literacy but also social and emotional development.

William Sweeney, PhD, is a professor and program coordinator in the Special Education Program at the University of South Dakota. Dr. Sweeney and Dr. Lisa Hazlett regularly collaborate on topics related to adolescent literature, students with disabilities, and inclusive practices in the general education classrooms, and on issues related to other diversity in our public schools. Dr. Sweeney is the author of many refereed journal articles related to topics involving empirically based interventions for students with special needs, behavior management and applied behavior analysis, as well as diagnostic and prescriptive classroom measurement approaches.

Barbara A. Ward, a clinical associate professor who teaches literacy and literature courses at Washington State University in Pullman, spent twenty-five years teaching English language arts in the public schools of New Orleans. She has been appointed to several different book award committees, including the Notable Books for a Global Society, the International Reading Association's Children's and Young Adult Book Award Committee, the Notable Children's Books in the Language Arts, the Amelia Elizabeth Walden Book Award Committee, and the Outstanding International Book Award Committee for the United States Board on Books for Young People. She reviews books in several venues, including The International Literacy Association's *Literacy Daily*.

Terrell A. Young is a professor of children's literature and literacy at Brigham Young University in Provo, Utah. Young's articles have been published in *Reading Teacher, Language Arts, Childhood Education, Reading Psychology, Journal of Children's Literature, Dragon Lode,* and *Book Links*. He is the coauthor or editor of seven books. Young served as president of the Washington Organization for Reading Development, the IRA Children's Literature and Reading Special Interest Group, and the NCTE Children's Literature Assembly. From 2009 to 2012, he served as a member of the IRA board of directors. Young is a recipient of the IRA Outstanding Teacher Educator in Reading Award.